RUNNING ON
RED DOG ROAD

Every once in a while, a voice comes along that makes you yearn for a childhood you never lived. Author Drema Hall Berkheimer invites you to skip along with her, big sis Vonnie, and best friend Sissy into the coal mining hills and hollers of West Virginia, at a time when gypsies and hobos were as common as doctors who made house calls.

KATHLEEN M. RODGERS, award-winning
author of *Johnnie Come Lately*

Running on Red Dog Road took me away to a time and a family that I will never forget. Drema Hall Berkheimer is a masterful, joyful, humorous storyteller who is just getting started. What a great book.

FAWN GERMER, International Speaker and
Oprah-featured bestselling author

Time and again I have been carried away by these stories, by the observations of a very shrewd little girl of her elders, both wise and the foolish. But don't let the sly humor fool you. Like the West Virginia coal country Drema Berkheimer writes about so affectionately and beautifully, there is always something going on here just beneath the surface, something grave, firmly rooted, even eternal.

BILL MARVEL, author of *The Rock Island Line* and
(with R. V. Burgin) *Islands of the Damned*

Drema Hall Berkheimer is a pure storyteller, one of the most wonderfully gifted I've ever read. As they make their way through *Running on Red Dog Road*, readers will smile continually, laugh out loud occasionally, and turn misty-eyed at times of joy or sadness as this child of Appalachia shares so lovingly her growing-up experiences with her cherished family and friends. Her phrasing is so exquisite and her words so perfectly chosen that her writing is a mixture of prose and poetry. It's best read in private, so there will be no distractions as the reader travels hand in hand with the author from beginning to end.

DR. GEORGE T. ARNOLD, Professor Emeritus,
W. Page Pitt School of Journalism and Mass
Communications, Marshall University

Running on Red Dog Road is an American treasure. Echoes of Mark Twain resonate in Ms. Berkheimer's tales of life in West Virginia in the care of loving and wise grandparents while her widowed mother helps save the world as a Rosie the Riveter. This family is an icon of what we should wish to be. Truly a needed voice in our world.

JULIANNE MCCULLAGH, author of *The Narrow Gate*

I *love* this memoir. The voice is masterful. Berkheimer layers into a perceptive child narrator an understated love of her family, a sassy streak that dodges consequences, and a precocious questioning of the society that surrounds her.

ROBIN UNDERDAHL, coauthor with Anshel Brusilow of *Shoot the Conductor: Too Close to Monteux, Szell, and Ormandy*

A competent historian could get the details right about mid-century Pentecostal Appalachian culture, but only Drema Hall Berkheimer could set us right in the middle of it. Through the eyes of a little girl who doesn't miss a thing, we experience spicy stew in the gypsy camp, and creative avenues to intoxication, and river baptisms. If the child Drema's observations could not always be shared with her grandparents, they are now shared with us. That will be to the delight of every reader.

DR. DOUGLAS M. GROPP, member, International Team of Editors of the Dead Sea Scrolls; Academic Dean, Redeemer Seminary

A sweet, whimsical, and often touching account of the author's childhood during a kinder, gentler era. It triggered great nostalgia during my reading.

DR. WILLIAM L. GROSE, retired NASA scientist and Assistant Director of Atmospheric Sciences, NASA Langley Research Center

In this gem of a book, Drema digs deep into her memory pool to bring forth images of well-developed places, characters, and things. In this highly technological age, we need this story to understand how ordinary people survived, thrived, and endured.

NJOKI MCELROY, PhD, storyteller, performance artist, and author of *1012 Natchez: A Memoir of Grace, Hardship and Love*

RUNNING ON RED DOG ROAD

AND OTHER PERILS OF AN APPALACHIAN CHILDHOOD

DREMA HALL BERKHEIMER

ZONDERVAN

Running on Red Dog Road
Copyright © 2016 by Drema Hall Berkheimer

Requests for information should be addressed to:
Zondervan, 3900 *Sparks Dr. SE, Grand Rapids, Michigan 49546*

Library of Congress Cataloging-in-Publication Data

   Names: Berkheimer, Drema Hall.
   Title: Running on Red Dog Road : and other perils of an Appalachian childhood /
      Drema Hall Berkheimer.
   Description: Grand Rapids : Zondervan, 2016.
   Identifiers: LCCN 2015036829| ISBN 9780310344964 (softcover) | ISBN
      9780310344988 (ebook)
   Subjects: LCSH: Berkheimer, Drema Hall — Childhood and youth. | Christian
      biography — West Virginia — Beckley.
   Classification: LCC BR1725.B438 A3 2016 | DDC 975.4/73042092 — dc23
   LC record available at http://lccn.loc.gov/2015036829

Published in association with the Loiacono Literary Agency, LLC, 448 Lacebark Drive, Irving, TX 75063

Cover design: Faceout Studio, Charles Brock
Interior design: Denise Froehlich
Author photograph: Bill Hall

First printing February 2016 / Printed in the United States of America

In Loving Memory
of
Grandpa, Reverend Luther Clevland Cales
Grandma, Clerrinda Adkins Cales

Father, Hursey Lee Hall
Mother, Iva Kathleen Cales Hall
Aunt, Lila Lora Cales Landwehr
Brother, Hursey Clev Hall
Sister, Yvonne Elaine Hall
and
of the little girl I once was
Drema Arlene Hall

Contents

The scales would drop from my eyes;
I'd see trees like men walking;
I'd run down the road against all orders, halooing and leaping.

ANNIE DILLARD, PILGRIM AT TINKER CREEK

A Note from the Author

Running on Red Dog Road is a memoir of my child-hood, mostly set in 1940s East Beckley, West Virginia. It is a living history of the Appalachia I lived in and loved as a child. How it looked and sounded and tasted. How it was. I was as faithful to those places and people as memory and the passage of time would allow—to do less would be a disservice to the remarkable family and place this book is meant to honor. Although names of all family members and many other characters are real, identifying character-istics of some places and people were changed to ensure their privacy. The stories in Running on Red Dog Road were recreated, not exactly as they were, for that clearly would not be possible, but as seen through my eyes as a child. As I wrote, I asked myself the same question over and over—what would Grandma think? I think she would be pleased. Mercy me, she'd say, here you've gone and set us down in a book. Yes ma'am, I'd say. I hope I have done her and all the others proud. Their influence on my life was and is immeasurable.

Begun as a legacy to my progeny, Running on Red Dog Road ended as a tribute to their forebears, the family to whom I owe everything. It is, then, a book of atonement. Resurrecting the dead, living with them, and burying them again was profoundly moving. It took me six years to complete this book, and for several of those years I wrote nothing at all—blindsided by memories that struck me dumb. They were mostly good memories, deeply rooted in family and mountains and the culture of Appalachia, so I was unprepared for the emotional physical spiritual toll this writing could and did exact—and puzzled too. After all, I come from stoic stock, not given to unseemly histrionics. I took after this kin, or so I claimed. I never cried. Not at my grandpa's funeral, nor my grandma's many years later. Not at my sister's or brother's or mother's. So the tears that overcame me as I relived our lives on that red dog road so long ago were an enigma—that is, until I realized every family member I wrote about is dead. Except for me. And the heartbreak is they died not knowing how I felt about them. They couldn't have. Until I began to write their stories, I didn't know myself.

RUNNING ON RED DOG ROAD

Prologue: in the beginning . . .

Her life traces a thin red line across a monitor in the intensive care unit. Tangled wires and tubes curl around baby arms and nose and foot. The widow's peak of dark hair that shapes her face into a valentine is shaved to make room for yet another needle. Each determined gasp heaves her ribcage up and down, forcing oxygen through lungs not yet ready to breathe.

She fights hard, this first grandchild of mine, and gradually recovers from the hyaline-membrane disease afflicting her at birth, earning her stripes early as the fifth living generation of strong women in her family. She is given her great-great-grandma's name, my grandmother's—Clerrinda—and like that grandma, she is called Rindy.

One year later, when Rindy is not only breathing but thriving, we have a picture taken for Grandma Clerrinda's one hundredth birthday. Five generations line up in front of the camera— Grandma, my mother, me, my daughter, and Rindy, on her great-great-grandmother's lap.

Still the strongest link in the chain, Grandma directs the photographer and us as well. He's from the newspaper and is gathering information for the feature article he's writing about her. She remembers everything, prompting us when we need help with a name or date.

Like a movie star, she talks and laughs and sings hymns into the video camera recording the event. She wears the dress I bought for her at Neiman's, a silk jersey print of mauve flowers with Irish lace trim. I overspend because I believe it might be her last new dress, her last birthday. I watch as she smooths the skirt over her lap. She thinks she looks beautiful, and she is right. She tells me she wants to be buried in that dress. Three and a half years later, her wish is granted.

But now, Rindy is a young woman, dandling her own baby on her lap. This great-granddaughter, called Drema after me, will carry the Appalachian name my father gave me deeper into the future than I can see. Rindy holds the old picture of the five generations in one hand, turning it this way and that, trying to recognize something of herself in her great-great-grandma's century-old face.

"Am I anything like the grandma I'm named after? Did you know my grandpa? Do you remember them?"

"Yes," I say, "I remember them."

I Come from Coal

We were in the middle of a war. Grandma came right out and told me, but I knew it anyway. Grandpa couldn't turn on the radio without us hearing how Uncle Sam needed everybody to buy War bonds, and ever last one of us had a brother or uncle or neighbor over there fighting, as everybody said, the Japs. Grandma told me it did not matter one iota to her what everybody said, I was to say Japanese.

And I did. At least when she was listening.

Grandma was busy fashioning an apron to cover up the shiny bronze bosoms on the Venus de Milo lamp Mother had mailed home in a big box from New York where she worked making airplanes for the War.

"Is my father off fighting in the War?" I asked.

"No, your daddy was a coal miner, but he wasn't lucky enough to get out of there alive."

"What happened to him?"

Grandma looked up from the pink-flowered scrap in her hand and studied me before she answered. "I reckon if you have a curiosity about him, you're old enough to know." I reckoned so too—after all, I had just turned four years old.

Grandma folded her hands on the table to show I had her full attention.

"A loose coal car ran over him down in the mines and killed him," she began. "You weren't but five months old and don't remember it, but make no mistake, you come from coal. Scratch any West Virginian a few layers down and you're bound to find a vein of coal. Yours runs deep. You were born in a coal camp at Penman, West Virginia, on November 17, 1939. I helped you into this world. Good thing. By the time the doctor came you'd been looking around all big-eyed for more than an hour. He weighed the heft of you with both hands, judging you to be better than eight pounds."

She turned to rifle through a drawer of old pictures, handing one to me.

"This is your daddy in his mining garb. His name was Hursey Lee Hall."

In the picture she shows me, my father has platinum-blond hair and a hint of a smile. There's something familiar about him, but I can't place what it is. His belt buckle skews off to the side. He wears a carbide lantern helmet, carries a dinner bucket in his hand. Maybe somebody took that picture on the very day he died, but there's no way for me to know.

Grandma said a big shot from the coal company came the morning of the funeral and gave my mother one thousand dollars for my father's twenty-nine-year-old life.

Then he gave her two days to move out of the sorry little company house we rented.

On the third day another miner would move his family in and take over my father's life, every morning riding a coal car over the soon-forgotten bits of him left splattered along rails down in the mines.

Mother used the money as a down payment on a house at 211 Fourth Avenue, East Beckley, West Virginia. Fourth Avenue was a red dog road. Red dog is burned out trash coal. If the coal had too much slate, it was piled in a slag heap and burned. The coal burned up, but the slate didn't. The heat turned it every shade of red and orange and lavender you could imagine. When the red dog on our road got buried under rutted dirt or mud, dump trucks poured new loads of the sharp-edged rock. My best friend Sissy and I followed along after the truck, looking for fossils. We found ferns and shells and snails, and once I found a perfect imprint of a four-leaf clover.

"Don't you be running on that red dog road," Grandma hollered as I ran off to play.

"Yes ma'am," I said over my shoulder.

And I'd mean it, but I could never slow my feet to a walk for very long. The scars on my knees are worn as permanent penance.

After the War ended, some of our streets were renamed in honor of men killed in battle, and Fourth was changed to Bibb. East Beckley was the divide between the doctor-lawyer-merchant-chiefs who lived in big houses in Beckley proper on streets like Woodlawn or North Kanawha, and the others who lived along the dirt road of the Gray Flats in scattered houses grimed by coal dust. From my house it was only down the road a few houses to Sissy's, then across the field to the 19-21 Bypass, the paved road that separated East Beckley from the Flats, where the road wasn't even covered with red dog.

There was a class system of sorts. We were somewhere in the middle.

Most everybody had a vegetable garden, called a Victory Garden during the War, and we did too. And we had a grape arbor and fruit trees. Like many of our neighbors, we had our cow Bossy for milk and butter, and a dozen or so chickens for eggs. The three pigs Grandpa fattened up and butchered every fall provided ham and bacon and pork chops. And we had pets too—a border collie named Queenie and an assortment of cats, my favorite a tomcat named Buttermilk. Sissy's grandma had a goat and ducks, and Mr. Lilly had honeybees. But we weren't out in the country. We were in a real neighborhood, with houses lined up on both sides of the road.

Built in the Craftsman style, our white two-story house had a blue roof and blue shutters, a front porch with a swing, and a scalloped, white picket fence all around. My grandma and grandpa moved to Beckley to live with us after my father got killed in the mines when I was five months old. They were left to take care of four-year-old me, my sister Vonnie, two years older, and Hursey, my eleven-year-old brother who was deaf, for a year and a half while my mother and Aunt Lila went off to build airplanes at a war plant in Buffalo, New York. I wondered how they got there. Maybe they rode the bus. Maybe they rode the train.

I couldn't remember when they left.

Every night before I went to sleep I tried to remember, but I never could.

Washed in the Blood

B est put in a jug of coffee and a quilt or two," Grandpa said. "Water's likely to be right chilly."

"There's quilts in the car and coffee's perking," Grandma answered.

Grandpa and Grandma started Cales Chapel, a church named after them, in the nearby mining town of Coal City in 1939, the year I was born. Grandpa preached there every other Sunday. Me and my sister Vonnie were going with them so Grandpa could baptize the people who got saved during the winter.

We climbed in the backseat among the quilts.

The mountain dropped off close to the edge of the road, sheering down through layers of hairpin curves so tight our old Buick headed back in the opposite direction every time we went around one. Vonnie felt carsick, so Grandma helped her climb over to sit in the front seat between her and Grandpa. Even my hard-to-turn insides felt uneasy when I looked at the steep drop only an arm's length away.

Grandpa caught my eye in the rearview mirror.

"Don't you worry none," he said. "We're a whole rabbit swerve from the brink."

I looked at my sister. Eyes half closed, she was nibbling a Saltine and sucking sips of lukewarm water from a fruit jar. Her blonde hair had sweated through and left a damp spot on the car seat. She had stuffed the end of one of Grandma's handkerchiefs in each ear to muffle the groan of the engine, giving her the look of a flop-eared bunny.

A *measly rabbit swerve.*

I craned my neck to peer over the edge. The sour that rose up burned my throat. I swallowed hard, trying to remember to breathe in through my nose and out through my mouth. We finally reached the valley and turned onto a narrow dirt road that led to a clearing. Grandpa pulled in next to somebody's beat-up truck and stopped.

I loosened my grip on the passenger strap I'd been hanging on to.

Dressed in a suit that had probably been baptized before, Grandpa waded three feet deep into the roiled-up river. A rope looped around his waist reached to a tree on the muddy bank, and half a dozen deacons tied themselves along the rope like rags on a kite tail. The new converts straggled into a loose line, waiting their turn to make their way out to Grandpa. Family and friends stood on the bank to lend support. Others came just to watch.

"I baptize you in the name of the Father and of the Son and of the Holy Ghost. Amen."

Grandpa leaned the good brother back until he was clear under the water. He came up shouting, "Amen!" and "Hallelujah!" Others came up gasping and spewing river water.

The brand-new washed-in-the-Blood-of-the-Lamb Christians dribbled up the bank and groped for raggedy towels to sop the water from their eyes. They huddled under quilts in the bed of a borrowed truck on the way back to the church, and I got to ride back there with them. Some just-cleansed soul started singing "Shall We Gather at the River," and others joined in. Somebody else tried to get "Are You Washed in the Blood?" going, but that one petered out after the first verse.

"Praise God," somebody said.

"Amen," somebody answered.

A thermos jug of coffee passed from hand to hand.

My grandpa and grandma belonged to the Pentecostal Holiness Church, and it defined them. It was a tough religion to live up to.

You had to pray a lot, read the Bible, and spread the word if you were Pentecostal. Grandpa particularly liked to spread the word. A retired coal miner turned evangelist by the time he appears in my memory, he spent every spare dime starting churches and holding revivals in neighboring towns, God and Grandma leading him every step of the way.

There were a lot of things you couldn't do if you were Pentecostal. You couldn't cheat or lie or steal or dance or chew tobacco or cuss. You couldn't act foolish. Of course, you couldn't drink or smoke or go to the movies or murder anybody or take the Lord's name in vain.

You couldn't wear feathers either. It said so in The Rules.

You couldn't gamble. Grandma wouldn't even allow cards in the house. I guess it was in case temptation got the best of me and I went to gambling all the Monopoly money away. She had reason to worry. Sissy had a pack of real playing cards with pictures of sailboats on the back. Sometimes we'd play gin rummy all night long. We'd eat a whole stack of Ritz crackers smeared with peanut butter and white Karo syrup, washing them down with red Kool-Aid. Next morning, Sissy's momma said it looked like a couple of little pigs had been rooting around in our bed.

"Why, that stuff's not fit to eat," Grandma said when I told her about the peanut butter and white Karo. She sniffed a little when she said it. She wouldn't have allowed crumbs in the bed, but I don't believe that had to do with being Pentecostal.

I reveled in the wrongdoing more than Sissy did because of gambling being such a big sin in my house. Her religion was easygoing about things like playing gin rummy all night.

She was a Methodist.

I decided I wanted to be a Methodist too.

Sissy invited me to go to church with her, and Grandma let me go since the Methodists were holding a service to honor the men who were off fighting in the War. The red brick church had a steeple with a big cross on top that lit up at night. Wine-red carpet

covered the floor, and candles burned on a long table in front of
the pulpit. The Methodists sang songs as foreign to me as if they
were in another tongue: "I Come to the Garden Alone," "Out of
the Ivory Palaces," and "Fairest Lord Jesus."

Three young men walked down the aisle to the front. All
were in uniform—one Army, one Navy, one Marine. They stood
stretched so tall it looked like they were trying to climb right out of
the necks of their uniforms and go home to their mommas again.

Mothers with sons overseas were asked to stand and some of
them were crying.

Sissy's preacher read out loud from Isaiah. *"But they that wait
on the Lord shall renew their strength; they shall mount up with
wings as eagles; they shall run, and not be weary; and they shall
walk, and not faint."* He talked some more, but he never did get
wound up like Grandpa. When he finished, we sang "Onward
Christian Soldiers" and "God Bless America." I knew the words
to those. We put our hands on our hearts and said the Pledge of
Allegiance while the men in uniforms saluted. One of the deacons
put out the candles with the back of a spoon.

Sissy's daddy took us by the Dairy Queen for a double cone
of vanilla with a curl on top. On the way home a spring shower
dimpled the dusty road. I stuck my head out the window and
opened my mouth.

Soft summer rain fell on my vanilla tongue.

"I do not know why in the world you have such a time with bee
stings," Grandma said. "Wouldn't happen if you did what you were
told and kept your shoes on like any reasonable person because you
know perfectly well that Mr. Lilly's honeybees are all over the place
this time of year and now here you are with a foot swole up big as
your head and having to use a piece of kindling to hobble around—
are you listening to a word I'm saying?"

I pulled another splinter off my makeshift cane.

"Yes ma'am," I said.

I'd worn a mud poultice for an hour to keep the swelling down and draw the poison out. Now Grandma wanted to slather the sting with Vicks. She thought Vicks was the remedy for any bite or itch or sting, whether the culprit was chigger or mosquito, poison ivy or poison oak, honeybee or yellow jacket. Of course she used Vicks anytime I hinted of a sore throat or coughed a couple of times. If slicking me down from my neck to my belly button or stuffing it up my nose didn't work, she'd put a big spoonful of the salve in a basin of hot water, throw a towel over my head, and make me breathe the vapors. When all else failed, she'd have me swallow a glob.

"Might help some and won't hurt any," she'd say.

When I bloodied my leg shinnying up a tree or split my knee on the red dog road, Grandma reached for the brown bottle of iodine, using the stopper that came with it to paint great swaths of orange on my skin. As she swabbed, she blew on the hurt place to keep it from stinging. I still squalled. I hoped she didn't go for the iodine to doctor my foot.

Grandma forgot all about my sting when a siren blared into the night and drowned me out. We rushed to turn lights off and pull shades down. We yanked curtains closed. Although we hoped the blackout was just for practice, you never really knew. We didn't want a glimmer from a flashlight or candle to give away our position to Japanese airplanes that could at that very minute be circling overhead, ready to bomb 211 Fourth Avenue. We sat in the stairwell like we were posing for a family portrait, afraid to look in case we saw our fear reflected in Grandma's eyes.

"No need to be afraid, we're in the hands of God," Grandpa said. He led us in the Twenty-Third Psalm. *"Yea though I walk through the valley of the shadow of death, I will fear no evil . . ."*

About that time a signal sounded to end the blackout.

Grandma bustled about turning on lights and opening shades, and the shadow of death and the fear of evil were no longer upon us. Grandpa lit a fire in the stove and put the percolator on. Before long the plink, plink, plink of the coffee perking could be heard, and the smell filled the house.

"Come on down, Rindy, I've got your cup waiting for you," Grandpa hollered upstairs.

"I'm coming, Clev."

"Well, you might want to hurry it up—they's a letter from New York I clean forgot to give you because of that blackout putting us all in the dadgum dark."

"Clev, you know I don't like that word."

"Why, *dark* is a perfectly fine word," Grandpa said.

Grandma said for him to stop his foolishness and read the letter to her. Grandpa told her he thought she'd want to read it for herself, but she said she had left her glasses upstairs. He started reading, but it was too low for me to hear. I was tired from all the commotion, and although I tried, I couldn't keep my gritty eyes open.

The Color of India Ink

M y mother was coming home for a visit. You would have thought it was the Queen.

Grandma gathered old newspapers and vinegar water and set me and Grandpa to cleaning windows, him on the outside and me on the inside. She attacked the oak floors with Johnson's Wax and elbow grease while Grandpa and I slung the cabbage-rose carpets over the fence and beat the devil out of them. Any cobwebs hiding near the ceiling were brushed away with a broom covered with an old shirt that she'd cut the buttons off to use later.

After she washed and ironed the kitchen curtains, Grandma decided they wouldn't do after all, so she made new ones. She sent Grandpa to paint fresh whitewash up five feet on the fruit trees. It looked nice, and it kept the boring beetles out of the cherry and apple and plum trees that shaded the back yard. When she had a few minutes to rest, she pinned starched doilies on cardboard like butterfly specimens. And every time she caught me and Grandpa sitting down, she assigned us another job.

There was no escaping Grandma when she got to cleaning.

The car spraddled over the whole road. It was the same indigo blue color of the bottles of thick India ink we dipped our pens in to write line after line of whorls and loops in penmanship class.

"That's a Buick Roadmaster," Grandpa said. "I expect an automobile like that might cost a man a thousand dollars."

My mother was in that car.

She had a new gentleman friend, and he was in that car too.

The man went around to open the door for my mother. Her platform spike-heel shoes swung out first. She wore a Kelly-green suit that tapered at the waist then flared into a peplum. A matching green hat set forward on her head, the black veil fluffed a little. The red fox stole that draped around her shoulders snapped a toothless mouth onto its own bushy tail. Sparks of light flew from a jewel-studded watch pinned on her lapel. She looked like a movie star I once saw a picture of in *LIFE* magazine. Claudette Colbert maybe, although I'm not sure about the name. When she hugged me, I smelled the scent of gardenias.

The man's hair was thinning, and he had some extra weight spread all over his body. His smile was big and crooked and had a dimple stopping it at each end.

Mother told me to say hello to Leo Reinbold.

"Hello, Goldilocks," he said. "I put something for you in my suitcase. Let's go find it."

The something was a tiny gold locket shaped like a book. It had roses of pink gold on the cover. Inside was a picture of my mother and one of me.

Mother showed Leo the spare bedroom with the attached sunroom, the windows lined with Mother's collection of salt and pepper shakers. There were more than a hundred sets. Women put ads in the backs of ladies magazines, trying to collect a set from every state. Mother would send little moonshine jugs to a woman in Idaho who needed salt and pepper shakers from West Virginia, and she'd get a set of grinning Idaho-potato shakers back. I never heard of a woman who didn't hold up her end of the bargain.

Mother was looking for her favorites, miniature bottles filled with red wine some woman sent all the way from California.

But she was not about to find them in that sunroom.

I was sure of that because Vonnie and I had stolen them. We were planning to risk hellfire by drinking the swallow of forbidden wine and refilling them with grape pop before anyone was likely to notice. My sister lost her nerve but egged me on until I twisted a top off and tipped the bottle to my tongue. The taste was bitter, not at all the fizzy sweet I expected. I rubbed my tongue hard on my shirt sleeve, leaving a wide purple track that I knew would puzzle Grandma when she did the wash. When I screwed the cap back on, Vonnie and I couldn't match up the torn seal, so we hid both bottles, hoping we'd think of some way to hide our thievery. We soon forgot all about it.

Mother looked puzzled as she scanned her collection.

"Looky what Grandma made," I said, drawing her attention away from the missing shakers and onto Venus, now modestly covered with a pink-flowered apron. Mother reached to yank the scrap of cloth off, but Leo held a hand out to stop her.

"Let's leave it," he said. "I think pink suits her."

And so we did.

Before supper, Grandpa asked Leo if he wanted to go with him to milk the cow.

"Sure," Leo said, "I've never seen a cow in person before."

Grandpa and Grandma laughed and called him a city boy, and Leo laughed too.

We went on long country drives in the big car that smelled like brand-new shoes. We found the best homemade raspberry ice cream. We walked up mountains with no trails. Where icy water poured down the rock face of a cliff, we cupped our hands and drank from the mountain.

After Leo and my mother went back to New York, the house turned quiet and empty. I didn't remember it being so quiet before.

I overheard Grandpa say that Leo was a prince of a fellow, but he was a heathen. He didn't even come from a Christian family, not that they weren't likely fine folks.

Grandma agreed that *did* have to be taken into account. She didn't expect he'd ever win a beauty prize, but she sure did like him.

Grandpa said Leo told him he was in the diamond trade.

Grandma said well that explained the fancy watch pinned on my mother's suit. Why, Leo had to be twenty years older than her. And he was from New York City for goodness' sake.

They both prayed Mother would come to her senses.

And she did.

Leo tried to convince her to marry him and she considered it, but in the end she couldn't do it. "Some things thrive if you take them way off and transplant them," she told him. "But not us."

Our roots were in West Virginia.

And that's where we would stay.

Strung on Fine Wire

The women sitting shoulder-to-shoulder in the church pew in front of me were dressed as drab as church mice. Every dress or suit was black or navy or gray or . . . well, there wasn't another or.

"Why don't the church ladies wear pretty dresses and makeup and jewelry like my mother does?" I asked Grandma.

"Those things call attention," Grandma explained. "As for the makeup and the jewelry, painted-on beauty and artificial adornment can't hold a candle to the natural beauty God gave us."

I wasn't so sure about that.

The church ladies didn't seem so sure either. Some of them must have thought face powder didn't count, so they dusted it on with little regard to matching the tint to their complexions. I sometimes saw the telltale fallout on navy crepe-covered shoulders in the pew in front of me.

The women didn't wear shorts or pants or dresses cut below the collarbone or above the elbow or knee. Pentecostal women didn't show much skin. A few brave souls satisfied their vanity by wearing their hair upswept into fancy whorls and twists. On Mother's Day, and any other day that gave them an excuse, those same women decorated themselves with homemade corsages of flowers and ferns and ribbons, which was against The Rules. But to their credit, I never saw a one of them wear feathers.

Grandma didn't use perfume, but a time or two I saw her take the brown bottle of vanilla out of the cabinet and dab a drop behind her ears. Once I even saw her splash some on an old hand-kerchief and tuck it in the front of her dress. Some of the ladies wore Johnson's Baby Powder and Evening in Paris or Blue Waltz perfume. The scents diffused into an invisible cloud that moved with them as they busybodied across the one-room church in twos and threes.

Grandma stood out among them. Although only average in size, she was an imposing woman, and the other church ladies followed her lead. I never heard her raise her voice in anger; she never needed to—her bearing carried a certain authority. She never sat down at home without her Bible or some piece of mending in her hand. Idle hands are the Devil's workshop, she often said. Hard-working and soft-spoken, a leader—Grandma had the gift of grace.

She was of Scotch-Irish heritage, with fair skin, blue eyes, and dark hair that glinted with red in the sun. Like most Pentecostal women, my grandma's hair had never been cut. Fashioned into braids wrapped around her head or wound into a bun at the nape of her neck, it fell past her knees when she took it down. Between washings she used a gold brush inlaid with mother-of-pearl to brush a mixture of lemon juice and water through her hair, and I sometimes caught the scent of lemonade as she passed. The brush belonged to a dresser set with a matching comb, hand mirror, and clothes brush, plus a jar she used to hold big fat hairpins. Before she went to bed, Grandma plaited her hair into one loose braid, then she brushed the tangles out of my blonde pigtails and plaited my hair into one long braid just like hers.

Saturday night was different. Grandma wound sections of my hair around strips of rags. The next morning, after I'd had my oat-meal and put on my Sunday-go-to-meeting dress, she unwound the rags from my head. Curls as tight as a screen-door spring spiraled down my back. When she plaited my pigtails for school, she'd dip her fingers into sugar water to stiffen the braids so they wouldn't come undone.

Sometimes when I sweated, I got a little sticky behind the ears.

On the Sundays Grandpa didn't preach at Cales Chapel, we went to the one-room Pentecostal Holiness Church in East Beckley for Sunday-morning services, and then back for more preaching Sunday night, and again on Wednesday night for prayer meeting. The children sat in the back pew and the adults met up front. Every week we were supposed to memorize a verse of Scripture. Most of the kids said, "Jesus wept." After all, it was the shortest verse in the Bible. But Grandma saw to it I had a proper verse to recite every Sunday so the church ladies wouldn't have cause to wag their heads about her.

"Let not your heart be troubled . . ."

"For God so loved the world . . ."

"And I say unto you, ask, and it shall be given you . . ."

I got to thinking. That last verse couldn't be true. Grandpa and Grandma had more faith than anyone I knew, yet they didn't seem to get much of anything they prayed for, even though they never asked for anything for themselves. It seemed to me if God made that great big promise, He should stick to it and not try to wiggle His way out of it because He thought you didn't need it or it wouldn't be good for you. When I asked Grandma, she said God answers all prayers, but He doesn't always give you the answer you want.

Grandma always took up for God.

When Grandma's best friend, a jolly roly-poly of a woman, helped her plan a Home Missionary Society meeting, they laughed and carried on worse than me and Sissy. Her first name was Clovis, but Grandma called her Sister Wood. I thought it was funny she didn't call her by her first name, them being such good friends and all.

"Well, Clovis is a silly name," I said.

"Clovis is a perfectly fine name. Not a thing wrong with it," Grandma said. "You know," she said, changing the conversation, "this would be a fine day for you and your grandpa to go find us a tree. The Lord's birthday will be upon us before we know it."

"I do believe your grandma wants me and you out of her way for a while," Grandpa said.

"No such thing," Grandma said. "If I wanted rid of you, I could put you to doing a dozen things that need attending to around here. I expect that'd make the both of you disappear fast as a magician's rabbit. I'd let you pare these apples for me if I didn't know what the outcome would be. We'd end up with half the apple wasting on the peel and one of you missing a piece of finger."

"To my mind it's a tad too soon to be cutting a tree, but if that's what you want, no doubt we can find you one," Grandpa said.

"Well, you could scout one out," Grandma said, dumping the cut-up apples into a skillet sizzling with butter, brown sugar, vanilla, and cinnamon to make apple upside-down cake or apple pie filling, I wasn't sure which.

I was hoping for fried apple pies. Grandma made them by rolling out six-inch pie crusts, putting a spoonful or so of the apple mixture on one side, then folding the crust over and crimping it with the tines of a dinner fork. She'd fry the little pies in lard, sprinkle sugar over them, and wrap them in a twist of waxed paper. Vonnie and I each carried one to keep our mittened hands warm on the way to school, eating them after our lunch of sausage and jam biscuits.

I looked out the door to see if it had snowed yet, caught una-wares by the clenching bite of winter. The early morning sky had a thin, washed-out look to it, but there was no snow.

Grandpa followed me onto the porch. He turned his face up and sniffed the air. "Smells like it's gonna snow," he said, sniffing another time or two.

"What does gonna snow smell like?"

"Well, you tell me."

I wrinkled my nose and inhaled a little.

Grandpa took a deep breath. "Hard to describe, but there's something different about it. Brings to mind the skin of a green apple."

I tried it again, sucking my lungs full of the icy air and holding it until the cold forced it out of me in one big whoosh.

"Takes some doing, but you'll get the hang of it."

The cold clamped down inside my head for a few paralyzing seconds.

"Careful now, you don't want to get your brain froze up," Grandpa said, stuffing the legs of my snowsuit into Vonnie's outgrown galoshes.

The pine tree I wanted was too tall, and the one Grandpa picked was too short. He held his arm straight up in the air to show me how tall it could be. We looked until we found one that went just past his fingertips. Grandpa reckoned it would do. He cut it down and dragged it to the car. When we got home, we put the tree in the sitting room off the guest bedroom because it stayed chilly in there, putting the scraggly side to the back when we placed it on the stand.

Grandpa turned the tree another inch or so to the right and looked over at Grandma, who nodded approval. "Most everything's got two sides to it," she said, glancing sidewise to see if I was paying attention. "Make sure it's your good side you're showing to the world. Put your best foot forward."

"Yes ma'am," I said.

Grandma sat down, ready to pare another pan of the Golden Delicious apples I'd picked up from Sissy's yard, looking for recently fallen ones. The ground lay covered with rotting apples, most of them buzzing with crazed honey bees drunk on the fermenting fruit. We didn't have Golden Delicious apples because Grandma said they went bad too quick, but we had Jonathans and Winesaps and a sweet, hard-fleshed yellow apple that had dark freckles on the peel, but I didn't know the name of that one.

The apple turned in her hand as the knife, honed on Grandpa's razor strop, skimmed just under the gold skin. Vonnie and I watched the peel reel out in an unbroken curl that pooled on the floor at our feet. Before she could get to it, I snatched it up and threw it over my shoulder. Holding my hands over my eyes, I peeked through my fingers to see how it landed.

It was plain as day. A perfect S.

"That means you're going to marry Grant Slack," Vonnie said.

"Am not. He doesn't even like me."

"Then I reckon he'll just have to get used to you. Or it could be Steve Bibb. But no, it has to be the last name that starts with an S," she said, making up that rule as she went.

And so it was decided. I was to marry dark-haired and dreamy Grant Slack.

At least until I threw another apple peel.

Grandma said her mother's apple peels were so thin you could read a newspaper through them. I never thought to test Grandma's, but I'm sure they came close. It was a matter of pride not to leave a layer of apple flesh on the peel because that would be considered wasteful. Waste not, want not, is what Grandma always said.

Vonnie and I decorated the tree with delicate pearl beads strung on fine wire in the shape of crosses and stars, ornaments brought over by Grandpa's German forefathers and passed on to him by his mother, Sarah Ellen Wiseman, who died in our spare bedroom when I was too little to remember. The angel on top of the tree had no legs, but a cardboard tube under her white satin dress fit over the tiptop branch. Along with the big family Bible, the nativity scene was set up on the library table next to a stand that held a Webster's unabridged dictionary almost as big as me.

Grandma let me and Vonnie help her make gingerbread men with raisin eyes and molasses cookies sparkled with sugar. We packed some of the cookies in a box of popped corn addressed to Mother and Aunt Lila in New York, and sent another big box addressed to "USA ARMED FORCES OVERSEAS."

Grandpa said he'd do his part by helping us eat the rest.

My mother couldn't come home for Christmas because President Roosevelt needed her to stay in New York and build airplanes for the War.

A big box waited at the post office. Grandpa pulled me there
in my red wagon, but the box rode in my place on the way home.
When I opened it Christmas morning, it was full of presents
wrapped in red-striped paper, each with a candy cane on top.

All except two of the presents were from Santa. There was a
china-faced doll with eyes that clicked open when you picked her
up, a blue-plaid skirt with pleats and a fuzzy angora sweater to
match, a set of watercolors in a tin container, new underpants with
the days of the week embroidered on them, flannel pajamas with
feet, a set of books with pictures and stories, and a wooden puzzle
map of the United States. I named the new doll Iva Kathleen after
my mother and placed her in a dresser drawer with several other
fancy dolls that she and Aunt Lila had sent from New York. They
were only taken out for an occasional well-chaperoned buggy ride
around the yard or to get their picture taken. They weren't the kind
of dolls who would sit beside you on the dirt and help you make a
windowsill full of mud pies. They lived sheltered lives that didn't
include dirty hands and bare feet. I liked my old doll Peggy better.
She didn't mind having mud on her underpants, a scabby nose, and
skint-up knees.

Peggy lived barefoot and fancy free. She took after me.

I sat on the floor, turning the forty-eight states face down until
I could recognize each by its shape. New York, where my mother
was working, didn't look all that far away from West Virginia.
Somehow I liked knowing that. When Sissy came by, showing
off the puffed wax lips she'd bought at Calloway's store, I saw an
opportunity to get them for myself. I'd have to hurry though, before
she decided to wear them. She was biting the tops off tiny paraffin
bottles and sucking out the green or red sugar water that was supposed to resemble soda pop but didn't.

"Bet I can name more states by their shape than you can,"
I said.

"What you got to bet?" Her eyes narrowed.

"My Mallo Cup against those dumb wax lips?"

It was a gamble, but she went for it.

I wore the pouty red lips around the house, admiring myself in every mirror I passed before chewing the fake mouth into a waxy gob. I don't believe I swallowed, but I may have.

To ease my guilt, I gave Sissy half of my Mallo Cup.

But not the biggest half.

My present from Aunt Lila that Christmas was a ten-carat-gold ring with a topaz birthstone. It fit perfect on my middle finger. I saved the present from my mother for last—a lavender blue music box cushioned in layers of tissue paper. I turned it over to wind it up. A silver label said the song it played was called "Clair de Lune." I listened to it every night before I went to sleep.

It was my lullaby.

5

Forcing the Forsythia

The ground still had Christmas snow on it when Grandpa left to go back in the mines. Grandma sent him off with a dinner bucket of sausage biscuits, a thermos of steamy potato soup, and three leftover gingerbread men who were missing a couple of eyes. She looked worried to me but she didn't let on.

"Why does Grandpa have to go back in the mines?" I asked.

"It won't be for long," Grandma said, brushing crumbs from the table with a whisk broom. "Just a few months so's he can qualify for a little pension coming in every month."

Grandpa was retired, and he was sick with silicosis, or black lung, as some had started to call it, which made him cough real bad. But once more he'd have to go down into the dank of the mines and breathe coal dust into lungs already turning to charcoal.

"That doesn't make sense," I said.

"No use to try," Grandma said. "There's no sense to be made of it."

At the end of the day, Grandpa returned—grit in the corners of his eyes, his graying hair turned dark again with the oily dust. Many days he had to work low coal, veins in mountain tunnels too low for a man to stand upright.

Stopping outside the gate, he hacked a sharp-edged cough into a big kerchief pulled from a pocket in his bib overalls. He walked up the porch steps, still bent in the shape of the mines, working his mouth to form a smile.

One day not long after, Mother walked right in and surprised us. She was home for a whole month, she said, because the airplane plant where she worked in New York had closed to get ready to build a different plane. "Nobody left there but a skeleton crew to get the place cleaned out," she explained.

I pictured bony people sweeping the floors and dusting propellers, all of them wearing red bandanas tied around their hairless skulls.

Aunt Lila got put on the skeleton crew, so she'd had to stay. At least that's what Mother told us. Although it wasn't a lie, it wasn't the whole truth either. Aunt Lila *was* working the skeleton crew, but the real reason she didn't come home was that she had got herself married to a New York fellow by the name of Eddie Kamphey. We weren't supposed to know a thing about it, but we did. We knew lots we weren't supposed to, but we never let on.

Mother burst in the back door, bringing with her the cold March air and a basket filled with whip-like branches.

"What are you doing with all those switches?" I asked, wondering if she was putting up a supply for the winter.

"They aren't switches," she said with a laugh. "They're branches from a flower bush. I'm going to show you how to force the forsythia."

"What does that mean?" I asked.

"Don't get ants in your pants," she said. "I'm going to show you right now."

I watched her pare the bark from the bottom four or five inches of each branch and place the whole bunch in a tall blue vase. "Feel here," she said, her finger gingerly running mine over a bud just beginning to swell. "The buds need to feel like that before you cut the branches. Now you go put some wrist-warm water in the vase. Make sure it covers up the bare part."

The spigot ran bone-cold at first, gradually turning warm to hot. I held my wrist to the stream of water and closed my eyes, all the while slowly turning the faucet to cool the water. When I couldn't feel it hot or cold, I filled the vase an inch or so past the stripped off bark and carried it back to Mother.

She nodded approval. "Now put it in the sitting room where it'll be out of the way."

"What about forcing the forsythia?"

"Be patient," she answered. "That comes later."

It was only a few weeks until Easter. To celebrate Christ rising from the tomb and Grandpa from the mines, Grandma said she figured she had enough butter-and-egg money saved up for him to get himself a new suit.

We watched out the kitchen window until the tailor finally got off the city bus up on Worley Road and walked down the red dog road to our house. He carried a beat-up leather satchel stuffed with drawings and swatches and chalk and a measuring tape.

We all gathered in the front room to watch. After careful deliberation, Grandpa chose the perfect cut and fabric and fit. The tailor measured and pinned and jotted and measured some more, muttering foreign words through a row of pins bobbing up and down in his mouth. Grandpa's new suit would be the dark-gray pinstripe worsted-wool three-piece double-vent cuffed-trousers notched-lapel model, with a watch pocket in the vest.

After the tailor left, I watched as Grandma poured Argo starch powder from a maroon cardboard box into boiling water, stirring until it was thick and shiny. She dropped a shirt into the pot, poked it down with a big wooden fork, then fished it out and dropped it into a metal tub until it was cool enough to wring and hang out to dry. The long, double clothesline sagged with a week's worth of just-washed clothes.

"We are either the cleanest bunch on earth or the dirtiest," Grandma said.

I believe she was leaning toward the dirtiest.

I curled up in the swing, looking at Rosie the Riveter on the cover of a brand new copy of *The Saturday Evening Post*. They should have put my mother on that magazine.

The shirts on the line flung empty arms into the wind until the rigor mortis of the starch set in. Off to one side, Grandpa's khaki workpants did a stiff-kneed country jig, one knee up then down, up then down, then kick way out. The warm wind died down. Lightning bugs blinked Morse code back and forth in the dusk.

"Come wash up," Grandma called out from the back door into the lavender twilight. "And don't be dawdling."

"Yes ma'am," I said.

After supper Grandpa got out his wood shoe-shine box and began to polish his black wingtips with a little spit and a can of black polish so intoxicating the Pentecostals might have outlawed it if they'd known about it. Once the polish dried, he whipped a felt-covered brush back and forth to coax out the shine. He held the shoe up to let me see myself reflected in the mirrored depths.

Grandpa's face reflected darkly behind my lighter one as he held the shoe in front of our faces. I watched as he put his shoe-shining kit back in order, the polishes and brushes and cloths lined up just so. For the first time I noticed his black hair was thinning and a little gray showed in the mustache he always wore. Although he was strong from working hard all his life, at five feet seven or eight and one hundred fifty pounds soaking wet, as he said, Grandpa wasn't a big man, yet he stood like a giant in my eyes. Although I wanted to be just like him, I looked closely and could not find a single feature to match up with one of mine. And yet I knew that if you skinned us inside out, you'd find we were both stuffed full of peach pancakes and thick bacon from breakfast and the blood that ran through him ran through me and joined us like only people in your family can be, and not all of them even, and not all the time. But me and Grandpa were. He taught me that the places and people we come from sear into our very being and follow us all the days of our lives. That faith and family twine around our limbs like grapevines. That they are the ties that bind.

On Easter Sunday morning Grandpa put on his new worsted wool suit and clamped elastic suspenders to his pants front and back. Garters, a strange contrivance of wide maroon elastic bands, were fitted above his calf and clipped to his socks to hold them up. A round watch attached to a gold chain draped across his chest and disappeared into the watch pocket in his vest. His shirt was starched, his shoes shined, his hat and his Bible in his hand.

Grandpa was armed to fight the Devil.

Holding himself still behind the walnut pulpit, Grandpa waited for his congregation to settle. He started quiet, but as voices from here and there in the pews began to encourage him with shouts of "Amen!" and "Praise God!" and "Thank you, Jesus!" his voice rose to a crescendo I likened to the voice of God. Oh, he could work up the congregation with fearsome warnings of the fire and brimstone awaiting those who didn't repent. He was awful longwinded though, so I was glad when the cadence slowed and I knew he was winding down. Soon he'd call for everyone to stand and sing Hymn No. 164, "Blessed Assurance," or maybe he'd announce Hymn No. 87, "Lord Lift Me Up to Higher Ground."

The Pentecostals weren't too good at singing, but a few voices lifted true and clear over the drone and drag of the congregation, and I hear them still. "Precious Memories," "What a Friend We Have in Jesus," "Will the Circle Be Unbroken," and Grandma's favorite, "His Eye is On the Sparrow." "Rock of ages, cleft for me . . ."—I thought it said, "Rock of ages, Clev for me." Clev was my grandpa's name. So that was my favorite hymn.

There was praying too.

Grandpa would say, "Brother Riley Davis from over in Crab Orchard is here visiting his mother who's doing real poorly, and he asks us to remember Mother Davis tonight and lift her all the way up to Heaven to be healed by the Lord God our Master Physician.

"Brother Slade Williams, would you kindly take us to the Lord in prayer?"

The good brother would fall to his knees right there in the pew or in the aisle and begin to pray. Soon all in the congregation were on their knees, and they joined right in, everyone praying out loud.

The Pentecostals believed you got saved, then sanctified, then filled with the Holy Ghost, which meant some would receive the gift of speaking in tongues. The Bible talks about speaking in tongues a good bit, but to tell the truth, it made most people uncomfortable. It didn't seem a bit strange to me. But then, I knew the ones who did it. They were Grandma and Grandpa, and they were normal as the applesauce pie my grandma made for Sunday dinner.

"Clev, I do wish you'd mind the time when you're up there preaching," Grandma said. "The biggest part of us have our dinners in the oven and you going on until half past the noon hour means folks are going home to a meal that's likely not fit to eat."

Grandpa shook his head. "I hear what you're saying, Rindy, but there's no way for me to tell precisely when a sermon is going to end. Just no way."

"Well, think of something. You can't have all the womenfolk staying home because you don't let out on time. And that's exactly what they're threatening. Sister Wood told me so. The men are affected too, you know, because it's them that's eating a dried-out roasting hen for Sunday dinner."

They had this disagreement most Sundays on the way home from church. But Grandpa said there was no two ways about it; he had to preach until there was no more preaching in him.

Once we got home, Grandma hurried to put Easter dinner on the table while Grandpa stayed outside to see to it the animals were sheltered. The sky was gray, with snow still on the ground, not a lot, but enough that Grandpa hid the Easter eggs inside the house for me and Vonnie to hunt for after dinner. The day before, we'd spent all afternoon dying hard-boiled eggs with food coloring mixed with vinegar and boiling-hot water, first writing our initials on the egg-shells with the wax of a used birthday candle. The dye didn't color the wax, so our initials showed up plain as could be. We dipped the eggs in a cup of red or blue or yellow, then started mixing our own colors. Red with blue to make purple. Red and yellow for orange. Blue and yellow to make green. Finally, we dumped all the colors together and got a muddy shade of brown.

We'd been eating chocolate bunnies and jelly beans and marshmallow biddies from our Easter baskets since we got up before dawn to go to sunrise service. Grandma warned we'd spoil our appetites, but Mother said for goodness' sake, it was Easter. She took our picture on the porch. We are dressed in our Easter garb, everything brand new from the skin out. Grinning from beneath our Easter bonnets, we are holding the baskets, the fingers of our white cotton gloves stained from handling the eggs.

Mother set the table in the dining room the way Aunt Lila always did, draping three lace tablecloths this way and that over a blue flowered cloth. Aunt Lila had first done that because our biggest lace cloth still wasn't big enough if we had both leaves in the table. She got compliments, so she kept doing it. Now Mother had copied her. Mother used the best dishes—the white ones with blue windmills—and the silver-plated knives and forks she'd polished the day before with baking soda and vinegar.

Soon the table was loaded with baked ham and fried chicken, candied sweet potatoes, mashed potatoes and cream gravy, stewed rhubarb, green peas and pearl onions, corn custard, pickled beets, and deviled eggs, the whites dyed blue and green and lavender—all served up on big platters and in sparkling cut-glass dishes passed down from generations before. Mother made yeast rolls and warm wilted lettuce salad from the season's first tender leaves of Bibb lettuce and green onion shoots.

She motioned me over. "Go get that blue vase you put in the sitting room."

I'd forgotten all about it.

When I opened the door, a big bouquet of bright yellow flowers bloomed where there had been bare branches. I carried the vase to the dining room as careful as if the yellow flowers were real gold, placing it in the center of the table.

Outside big wet snowflakes mixed with icy drizzle, but inside it felt like spring. There were lace-trimmed anklets on my white patent-leather feet, "Sunday" embroidered in pink on my yellow underpants, bread pudding with warm raisin sauce to be spooned over it, and Easter eggs waiting to be found.

And Mother and I had forced the forsythia.

6

A Hobo's Prayer

The Pentecostal Home Missionary Society believed in helping your neighbor. My grandma believed everybody was our neighbor, and that included the hobos who hopped on and off trains that coughed and belched through our town, oily plumes of smoke and a mile of coal cars trailing between the black engine and the bright red caboose. Grandpa said he'd heard tell hobos had a way of marking houses known to serve up a good meal. Ours must have had a sign pointing right at it because every hobo traveling north in the spring and south in the fall found his way to our back door.

No one was ever turned away.

Wild-eyed and bushy-headed, the man leaning against our gate wore a rumpled Sunday suit that harkened back to better times, a white shirt that was nearly clean, and a tie so stained the original color was anybody's guess. Grandma went to the edge of the garden and hollered Grandpa's name. He hurried over and introduced himself, shaking the hobo's hand. He always found some chore for the hobo to do, even if it didn't make sense to me.

This time, he led the hobo to a stack of kindling near the stump we used as a chopping block. I watched as he gestured toward the cellar door. The man nodded and began to fill the wheelbarrow with the wood, the very same load another hobo had carried from the cellar door to the chopping block just a week or so before.

Grandpa always said a man that earned his own dinner could hold his head up.

Before long Grandma appeared on the porch, carrying a steaming plate of leftover pork chops and sweet potatoes served with biscuits and a tin of hot creamed coffee.

The hobo eyed the biscuits.

But he wasn't going to get fed quite yet.

Grandma offered a basin of water with a thin slice of lye soap, which scoured all the dirt and part of the hide off, leaving the hobo's hands pink as the pig snouts she'd made the soap from.

The hobo looked at the biscuits again.

But Grandpa said we should first bow our heads for a word of prayer.

"Lord, we just thank you for the bounty of this food we are privileged to share and for your many blessings on this family. And Lord, we ask you to bless this humble traveler. Protect and guide him as he goes forth across this great land. Lead him through the unknown trials and tribulations he's bound to face. But Lord, if it be Thy will, allow him the sweetness of some victories. In the precious name of the Father and of the Son and of the Holy Ghost. Amen."

All of us said, "Amen."

So the hobo said, "Amen," too.

"You sit down in the swing there and enjoy your meal," Grandma said over her shoulder, disappearing into the house and leaving me and the hobo for Grandpa to deal with. Grandpa busied himself raking leaves and giving me rides in the wheelbarrow to keep me from being an aggravation. I watched the man pick up his fork and load it with sweet potatoes. He didn't stop until the plate was clean.

Grandma came back out holding a paper bag. "I put some extra in here for you to take with you. Make you a good supper later on."

Courtly as he thanked Grandma for the meal, the hobo nodded to Grandpa's "God bless you" and headed off down the red dog road. He sang a ditty:

don't know where i'm going
don't know where i'll be
i'm at home in this fair land
from sea to shining sea my friend
from sea to shining sea.

Grandpa watched him go. "For the most part they're good men down on their luck," he said. "Times is hard for lots of folks nowadays."

I wondered out loud if hobos ever got lonely.

Grandpa thought on that before he answered. "For the most part, I'd reckon not," he said. "Funny how some men are content not putting a foot across the county line while others have the need to roam. You know how geese have it in them to fly south for the winter? Some men are born with that same yearning. Like the geese, it's in their blood."

Not long after, we had another hobo visit, this time at Sissy's house. Late one morning we were sitting on her maroon mohair divan cutting clothes out of an old Sears, Roebuck catalog to dress our family of paper dolls. Her momma had put her daddy in charge of us while she went downtown to shop for shoes. Sissy's momma was four feet ten inches tall and wore a size two and a half shoe, so she bought sample sizes when they went on sale. She looked even smaller next to Sissy's daddy, who was close to six feet tall and blocked most of the light when he stood in a doorway.

When someone knocked at the door, Sissy jumped up and ran to see who it was, the scantily clad paper dolls in her lap flapping wildly to the floor.

I thought she had lost her mind.

People rarely knocked on our doors. Those who did were people we knew, and they only gave a couple taps before opening the door and sticking their head in to holler was anybody home. If that didn't work and they had a mind to, they came on in and made themselves at home until somebody showed up. Now, Sissy did not have the faintest notion who was outside that door, and we'd both been warned about a million times not to open the door to strangers. A bowlegged little man stood there, his beat-up hat pulled down over his ears. Shorter by a good head than Sissy's momma and grimed from head to foot with coal soot, he grinned up at Sissy through gap teeth.

"Young missy, is the master of the house available for a word?"

"If you mean my daddy, he's in the bathroom," she answered.

The hobo was right about that master-of-the-house part. Sissy's daddy did rule the roost. Although he had a big wood paddle he called the Board of Education hanging on the wall, I'd never known him to use it. He didn't have to. A glance was enough to keep us in line. Sissy tried real hard to please him. So did I.

That's why it was a complete shock to my system when Sissy opened that door.

"Would you be so kind as to give a thirsty sojourner a cool glass of water?" the man asked.

"I'll go get you some," Sissy replied, "but you'll have to come in the house because my daddy won't allow me to let the door stand open."

The little man followed her in and hoisted his sooty self onto the couch, taking off his hat and stuffing it in a pocket. I noticed his forearm was tattooed with "A Mother's Love" and a tombstone with "R.I.P." on it. He'd washed his hands somewhere, and water had run down to his elbows, leaving clean tracks in the dirt on his arms.

Sissy's daddy, probably hearing the commotion, came into the room holding an unfolded copy of the morning *Post Herald* in his hand. He stopped dead in his tracks when he saw a real live dwarf perched on his couch, his feet sticking straight out, surrounded by me and Sissy and a bevy of half-naked paper dolls. I expected him to have a conniption, but he didn't.

I gave him credit for staying calm.

"The young lass was about to fetch me a cool drink," the man said. "I hope the mister doesn't mind."

Sissy's daddy nodded and told her to get the man a glass of water and to fix him a sandwich.

I couldn't believe she was getting off so easy.

The man talked between bites of the peanut butter sandwich.

I knew it was peanut butter because that's the only kind of sandwich Sissy ever made. If I had made a nickel bet on it, I would have won the money.

The hobo man was, or so he said, with Barnum in his day. Oh, he'd seen and done it all, traveled far and wide. He'd run off and joined the circus when he was but a lad of twelve. It was a hard-bit life, but he'd got used to it. First thing they'd put him to doing was shoveling steaming piles of dung out of the cages of the lions and tigers and elephants that performed in center ring. The boss man soon realized a dwarf was as much of an attraction as the beasts he was tending, so they put him in as a clown. The life of a nomad was all he'd ever known. Now he rode the rails where he could still watch the countryside go by. He liked waking up every morning not knowing where he was. When he needed a couple dimes to rub together, he could always pick up some change juggling on street corners. Plenty of people would drop a coin or two in his hat. Why, they'd pay a dwarf such as himself just to let them gawk.

When the hobo finished his sandwich, Sissy's daddy, who had hardly said a word, walked him to the door. He stood there for a minute, watching as the man headed down the road.

I'd been waiting for the hobo to show us some juggling, trying to picture how he'd manage it with such short arms, but he never did. I didn't blame him. Sissy's daddy didn't appear to be in a juggling kind of mood.

"You'd best run on home now," he told me. "Sissy can't play anymore today."

"Yes sir," I said.

I was somewhat relieved I didn't have to make up my mind about staying or going, but I admit to being concerned about what was going to happen to Sissy without me there.

The next day she told me she didn't want to talk about it. Begging didn't work, but once I promised she could keep my Sparkle Plenty doll all night, she gave in. I knew she would. She could not resist that Sparkle girl.

Yes, she admitted, her daddy did give her a spanking.

It was, to my knowledge, the only time he ever took that paddle off the wall.

"Did it hurt bad?" I asked, not sure if I hoped she'd say yes or no.

"Just stung for a minute. Three licks is all I got. One for opening the door, one for letting that little man come in the house, and another to make sure I'd never do it again."

"Did you cry?"

"Of course I did!" Her look was withering.

I didn't know whether to offer admiration or sympathy, so I kept my mouth shut.

Sometimes, when Vonnie was really pitching a hissy fit, Mother gave her a couple of swipes with a switch. That is, if she could catch her. I'd never been switched or paddled, although I'd come close a time or two. It's not that I never deserved a paddling, because I'm sure I did, but so far I'd wriggled out of it. Lots of my escapes were because I was the baby, with an older brother and sister who surely knew better and should have kept me out of trouble. Or so Grandma said. Nevertheless, I was trying to get a feel for how to act, just in case.

Hobos came from the north in the fall when they headed for warmer weather, and in the spring they headed back north, often leaving gifts made from cigar boxes or popsicle sticks or matchsticks. Sometimes a hobo would offer to paint a picture of your house on a board or a piece of cardboard for a few coins. Some used real paints, but others kept a little tin of watercolors in their hobo sack, which was usually an old pillowcase or tablecloth tied onto a pole. A hobo painted a picture of my friend's house that her mother liked so much she hung it up in their living room.

Grandpa came in the house with the *Raleigh Register* tucked under his arm. We had two daily newspapers. The *Post Herald* was the Republican paper and the *Raleigh Register* was for the Democrats. Grandpa was a Republican and Grandma was a Democrat. Since she was the one who ordered the paper and dealt with the paperboy, the *Raleigh Register* was thrown in our yard every afternoon. Sissy's family got the *Post Herald* early in the morning.

"Anybody remember that singing hobo fellow we fed a while back?" Grandpa asked. "Appears he's been by here and left us something. Found it wedged out there in the gate. Note says he's sorry he didn't catch us at home. He thanks us for the best meal he's had since leaving his mother's knee in Omaha. Rindy, you get credit for that," Grandpa said, giving a nod to Grandma. "Looks like he left us a poem."

"Read it to me," I said.

"Way I figure, the one wants it read is the one to read it." Grandpa handed the poem to me.

a hobo's prayer

smokedusting

wanderlusting
rails click by below
heard them once
heard them twice
calling me to go

stew ain't half bad
company's fair
not a soul i know
been here once
could be twice
time for me to go

they's kids somewhere
call me dad

names i hardly know
seen them once
or maybe twice
still i've got to go

down south the sun god
shines like gold
here it's about to snow
i been there once
or was it twice
oh Lord i loved it so

when heaven turns the
caged birds free
i watch them from below
just one more time
or maybe twice
sweet Jesus let me go

"Amen," Grandpa said.

Grandpa said that hobo had been given a gift and that we are all given one and some are given many.

"What's my gift? I asked. "You think maybe I could make a rhyme?"

"I wouldn't rightly know," Grandpa said, "but you won't know either until you try it. And that's something I do rightly know."

"What's your gift then?" I asked.

"Some folks seem to find their gift early on," Grandpa said. "I haven't thought much on it, but I reckon mine came to me late. After working the mines all them years, I got saved and sanctified and filled with the Holy Ghost and commenced preaching and starting up little churches here and there where folks didn't have any. I like to think I did some good."

"Amen," Grandma said from the porch.

The Spirit Is Willing

We hadn't had any more hobo visits, but my Uncle Ed, who'd arrived at our house earlier in the day, had stirred things up in his own way. Grandma found him balled up on the bedroom floor, spit dribbling from the corner of his mouth, arms hugging his knees. It looked like he was trying to keep his legs from shaking loose and flying off across the room. His teeth would have chattered if he'd had them in his mouth, but he'd put them in one of his shoes, for safekeeping, I guess. The other shoe was still on his foot.

Grandpa went to fetch the doctor while Grandma tried to wrest the truth out of her brother. It didn't take long. He'd decided, he said, to have himself a little toot of the rubbing alcohol we kept in the bathroom medicine cabinet.

Grandma's face turned pasty as biscuit dough.

"Good Lord have mercy, Ed, you must have lost your mind. Why, that stuff will kill you deader than a doornail. I declare, sometimes you act like you don't have the sense God gave a goose."

Uncle Ed commenced to nod his head to show he agreed with her about him and the goose. Grandma told him he better be praying that Grandpa came back with the doctor.

Uncle Ed had an even better idea.

"You say a prayer for me, Rindy. Tell Him I ain't such a bad feller. He's way better acquainted with you. He don't hardly know me."

"Edward Moore Adkins, I've prayed for you every single day of your life, and I'm not likely to up and quit anytime soon," she said.

Uncle Ed was Grandma's baby brother and the only one who visited us regularly because he only lived a few hours away. But he hadn't come for a visit this time. Their brother Teel had taken sick, and Aunt Annie had written for Grandma to come to Flat Mountain to help her. Since Grandpa was staying behind to tend to the animals, Uncle Ed would drive us there. He often smelled of alcohol, which gave Grandma cause for extra praying, but we needed the ride. Grandpa said the best way to deal with Uncle Ed was to keep hopes high and expectations low. But when Uncle Ed arrived just before dinner, even Grandma's highly trained senses didn't see or smell any signs of liquor.

That hadn't lasted long.

Between groans and grimaces, Uncle Ed tried to explain how he'd thought just a taste of the rubbing alcohol wouldn't hurt him any.

"That's all I had, Rindy, and that's the plain truth of it. I swear to God it is."

I watched for lightning to strike him dead, but God must have decided to let it go this time.

Grandma decided not to.

"Ed, mark my words, I will not tolerate you taking the Lord's name in vain in this house. And I will not tolerate you acting a fool and drinking the rubbing alcohol either." Her words were sharp, but ever so gently she smoothed his thinning hair back and folded a wet washrag over his forehead.

"You know, I was just recollecting how you bossed me around when we were young'uns, Rindy, and here you are still doing it all these years later." He somehow managed a feeble smile.

If Uncle Ed's car was off its feed, which meant he'd used up his gas ration, he'd ride the bus to our house. When Grandma spotted him making his way down our red dog road from the bus stop on Worley Road, she could pretty well judge how much he'd had to drink. If he was tipsy, he walked gingerly, as if he was trying to stay within the lines. But if he was soused, he reeled and tilted, flailing his arms like an out of control tightrope walker. On those occasions, Grandma would feed him and put him straight to bed to sleep it off.

Next day I'd sit with him on the grass while he told stories about some French girl he'd had a fling with in Paris during our first big war overseas. Grandma, who didn't know what he might say next, told him she'd heard quite enough, but he just threw his head back and laughed. She walked off, saying he wasn't getting another minute of her attention until he behaved.

He'd read the newspaper out loud, politics and sports and obit-uaries, finishing with the funny papers. Dick Tracy was our favorite. He'd hoot and holler and slap his leg at the antics of B.O. Plenty and Gravel Girty and their blonde-headed daughter, Sparkle Plenty. Uncle Ed said that Sparkle girl didn't have a thing on me, no sirree, not a thing.

He told me I was the spitting image of Lana Turner. He bet one day a Hollywood man would see me eating an ice cream cone in the drugstore downtown and make me into a big movie star like her. Uncle Ed said he'd come to see me, but I'd have to let him in for free. I cut a picture of Lana Turner out of the newspaper, hold-ing it up to my sun-speckled face in the mirror.

It was usually fun when Uncle Ed came, but this time I was scared. Grandma was doing what she could until the doctor got there. She hollered for me to bring the cream pitcher and a jar of milk from the refrigerator. After she emptied the milk into the half full pitcher of cream, she made Uncle Ed turn it up until he glugged the last of it down. He said he thought Grandma was right—he probably had killed himself, and as bad as his belly hurt he didn't much care. Grandma said no need to make matters worse by adding foolish talking to foolish acting.

"Trouble is, I'm not so sure Ed's acting," Grandpa said, coming in the door with the doctor behind him. "That foolish part sounds about right though."

Relief washed over Grandma's face when she saw them. Doc Cunningham had been our family doctor forever. His one-room office near the post office in East Beckley was furnished with cracked leather, faded linoleum, and generations of secrets. Shelves around the walls held olive and cobalt and amber bottles of pills and potions he doled out or mixed up, depending on what ailed you.

In the office Doc Cunningham carried a Persian cat draped around his neck like a boa, and white fur floated in the shaft of sunlight filtered through the dingy window. One day when Grandma took me there to pick up something or other, he told me the cat was called Pitty Sing after a cat in a play he'd once seen. It was called *The Mikado* if I ever wanted to look it up. I never forgot the name.

The ancient smell of the office soaked into everything it touched, and as he moved around our bedroom, poking Uncle Ed, whiffs of leather and liniment mingled with the smell of tobacco from a yellowed Meerschaum pipe he kept in his jacket pocket.

Doc Cunningham peered out of eyes skimmed over with age as he wiped wire-framed spectacles with a peach-colored hanky he'd borrowed from Grandma. He told Uncle Ed it looked as though his life had been spared for another day.

"Thank God for that," Uncle Ed said.

"Wouldn't hurt none," Doc Cunningham replied, "but to my mind you should thank your sister for that hearty dinner she fed you."

Grandma had made pork chops with cabbage, scalloped potatoes, fried apples, and cornbread muffins, with blackberry cobbler to finish off the meal. Uncle Ed could never get enough of his sister's cooking, so he ate extra helpings.

"You're mighty lucky," Doc Cunningham continued, "mighty lucky indeed. But touch your lips to that poison again and you'll not only be a damned fool, Ed Adkins, you'll be a dead one, and I'll come sign the papers over you to prove it." His drawn-down eyebrows squirmed like aggravated woolly worms.

Uncle Ed nodded that yes he was lucky and yes he was a damned fool. He announced he was giving up alcohol in all its evil forms. He had in mind to start preaching on the street corners downtown where some wayward soul might hear the Word and find eternal salvation. He'd give out those leaflets on the bus too, the ones that said, "ARE YOU SAVED?" or, "JESUS IS THE WAY." Maybe he'd knock on doors and witness to people right there in their own front rooms.

"I'm glad to hear it," Grandma said. "I always am, but I hope you really mean it this time."

Uncle Ed always repented and got saved after he got drunk, but it never took. Soon he'd be backslid again.

Grandpa said Uncle Ed had slid back and forth so many times he was bound to have wore the seat of his britches out. But God worked in mysterious ways, and you never knew when a man's heart would be changed. He'd keep praying for him long as it took. Like the Scripture said in Matthew, *"The spirit is willing, but the flesh is weak."*

Uncle Ed liked that verse and had Grandpa repeat it several times.

"I've got a feeling that one's gonna come back to bite me," Grandpa said, a grin tugging at his mouth.

Doc Cunningham had said "damned fool" right out loud in our house. Grandma didn't hear him because she was in the kitchen getting money out of her butter-and-eggs jar, so he didn't know about her no-blaspheming rule. While she was gone, Grandpa made Uncle Ed pay the two dollars for the doctor's house call. Although Grandma didn't look too happy about it, she took her two dollars back and put it in her apron pocket just the same.

She walked the doctor out on the porch to ask would Uncle Ed be able to drive the car the next day. Doc Cunningham said no reason not to as long as he stayed out of the rubbing alcohol. Grandma was so relieved she sent the doctor home with a quart jar of the pickled eggs he was so fond of.

"Well, that settles it then," Grandma said. "We'll leave before light in the morning." Her eyes gave Uncle Ed a quick once-over. "You look just fine to me, a little green around the gills maybe, but fine. I don't expect you'll feel any worse driving than not. Might keep your mind off your misery."

Uncle Ed looked stricken, but he didn't say a thing.

Grandma had put the quietus on him.

Only the Essence Remained

A little setback like Uncle Ed almost killing himself wasn't about to stop Grandma. She gathered a stack of clean quilts and feed sacks in a box, filling another with a cured ham and a big slab of salt pork. She packed canned peaches, blackberry jam, and jars of green beans, corn, and tomatoes into the last box, stuffing old rags between the jars so they wouldn't break. She filled two flour sacks with potatoes and apples and another half full of pinto beans. Grandma never went anyplace empty-handed.

We always had plenty of everything to share with family and neighbors and hobos alike. Food was put up for the winter, with rows of jars four deep lining the fruit-house shelves. Hand-sewn quilts were stacked to burrow under on cold nights, and more were being made on the quilting frame crowded into the kitchen. Feed sacks turned up as pillowcases and dishtowels and aprons. Grandpa would take me with him to buy feed for the chickens so I could pick out the sacks I liked. When Grandma ran the sturdy flowered prints through her Singer treadle sewing machine, rose and yellow and lilac sundresses flowed out the other side.

After I squeezed the last bit of Ipana from the tube, Grandma made do by using soda and a sprinkle of salt on my toothbrush, and if the bottle of Fitch's shampoo ran out, she washed my hair with Ivory soap. "Use it up, wear it out, make it do, or do without," I often heard her say.

But there was still a chicken in our pot.

And homemade dumplings too.

Grandma was taking me and Vonnie to Flat Mountain with her, leaving Grandpa to fend for himself and tend the animals. She finished up the packing, sending me to the fruit house for a quart of bread and butter pickles to fill an empty spot in one of the boxes. After checking on Uncle Ed, she started up to bed. Before long she came back down and headed toward the bathroom, reappearing with the bottle of rubbing alcohol safely tucked under her arm.

"Safe's a whole lot better than sorry," she muttered, and started back up the stairs.

Next morning Uncle Ed's complexion had improved to a gassy yellow, so we started before daylight, stopping along the way to get pint bottles of milk for him and nickel packs of peanuts and bottles of Orange Crush and Grapette soda pop for us. The sign on the ESSO filling station said gas was thirteen cents a gallon. Grandma said she expected we could get it cheaper on down the road apiece, but Uncle Ed pulled in despite her, telling the man to fill 'er up, and yes, he most assuredly could check the oil while he was at it. Grandma knew some battles weren't worth fighting, and since she was depending on Uncle Ed's good graces to get us there, she didn't let on she noticed.

Vonnie and I played cow poker, each of us counting cows in fields along our side of the road. If you passed a cemetery on your side, you had to bury all your cows and start over. Bushes or other lumps could be mistaken for cows, so lots of arguing and a fair amount of cheating went on until we aggravated Grandma so much she put a stop to the game. She handed us the shoebox that held paper dolls and coloring books with pictures of open-mouthed children frozen in place as they frolicked around a Maypole. When we lost interest, we looked for Burma Shave ads, six wood signs stuck in the ground along the roadside, each with a line of a poem.

This one had a word Grandma didn't allow me to say. I liked
it best:

SHE WILL FLOOD
YOUR FACE
WITH KISSES
BECAUSE YOU SMELL
SO DARN DELICIOUS
BURMA SHAVE

We turned off the highway onto a dirt road that drew itself up
the mountain in fits and starts, stopping for cattle gates that had
to be opened and closed before going on. We rounded a curve,
and the house appeared of a sudden, a grand place in a clearing of
piney woods halfway up Flat Mountain. A massive stone chimney
rose from the center of the house, which sat squat and square, a
moat-like porch encircling the whole place. Homemade rockers
were scattered all around, and I counted four oversized picnic
tables with trestle benches, one on each side of the porch. At each
corner, a swing hung kitty-cornered so you could look out on the
sunrise or sunset depending on what you fancied at the time.

Uncle Ed said he didn't know why in tarnation a body would
want so many tables and chairs.

"Teel always did like a lot of company," Grandma said.

Inside the house, pine shelves lined the walls. Plates stood
along the back of the lower shelf, with baskets and tins filled with
kitchen needs in front. Below the bottom shelf, hooks held iron
pots and skillets. All the rooms had shelves—the ones in the bedroom held a sewing basket full of wooden spools of thread, folded
clothes, rows of books, a jar of buttons, and an assorted collection
of empty mason jars. Hooks underneath held a double-barreled
shotgun. Three print dresses and one of navy serge hung next to a
man's black gabardine suit that had a curious long jacket.

A celadon-green Hoosier cabinet sat against one wall. Another
piece I admired was a walnut trunk that had flowers and birds

carved all over. Uncle Teel made that trunk for her as a wedding present, Aunt Annie said, and she used it to store her fancywork. She tilted up the lid to show us. From the looks of it, Aunt Annie spent all her spare time doing fancywork. The trunk was almost full, and doilies and antimacassars decorated every chair and table. I wouldn't have been surprised if Uncle Teel's long johns had morning-glory vines embroidered around the back flap.

The house had a place for everything and everything was in place, just the way Grandma liked, yet there was an unsettling smell of stale cooking odors and the fetid stench of an ever-present chamber pot. The air felt heavy, and what got to your lungs seemed all used up. Not a whiff of fresh air could enter because Aunt Annie had all the windows and doors shut up tight.

Grandma took one look around, and told Aunt Annie not to worry herself another minute—she'd set things right in no time. She banished the chamber pot to a far corner of the porch, then opened up every window, letting sunlight flood in and the fresh breath of the mountain blow through. She put a pan of water and spices on the stove, and soon the aroma of cinnamon and cloves and vanilla wafted through the rooms, mingling with the piney scent of the woods.

"Leave that pan on the stove, and I expect it would freshen up the house every time the fire's lit," Grandma said. She was at her best when she was telling other people what to do. Somehow they'd end up thinking it was their own idea and weren't they just smart as a whip to have thought of it.

After Aunt Annie washed Uncle Teel head to toe, she rubbed Jergen's lotion over his bony frame and put him in a clean suit of long underwear. She and Grandma helped him into a chair on the sunny side of the porch, putting a pillow behind his head and tucking his favorite crazy quilt around him.

A crazy quilt was made from leftover fabric scraps of different sizes and shapes and colors put together in a patchwork design. Grandma had one at home that her mother, Sarah Jane Adkins, had made—every piece embellished with embroidered flowers and initials and names of family members. Grandma said it looked like her mother had used up every stitch she knew and then made up a bunch more. She told me that quilt would be mine one day since I admired it.

There was nothing much in the house to eat, so Grandma put a big pot of the pinto beans she'd brought from home on the fire, seasoning them with wild ramps and a chunk of salt pork and adding a handful of mustard greens from the garden. When the beans were done, she took a cup of the savory broth out to the porch where Uncle Teel was resting.

Five inches past six feet tall, his rawboned frame had muscled over from working outdoors as a lumberman from the time he was an overgrown thirteen-year-old. His hands, knobbed at the knuckles and wrists from hard work, were still big and rough as bark, but the rest of him had shriveled down so only the essence remained. Grandma made dandelion tea for him, stirring in a spoonful of molasses to fortify his blood.

Comforted, Uncle Teel napped in the warmth of the sun. When the lavender dusk darkened into purple, Aunt Annie and Grandma came out and sat with Uncle Teel, now awake. They promised him he could stay on the porch as long as he wanted the next day. Finally, he let them help him to his bed. I heard Grandma praying to God to give His child Teel the peace that passeth all understanding.

"Amen," Aunt Annie said.

9

Mistook for a Haint

I woke up to Grandma clattering around the kitchen, then her footsteps headed toward the bedroom Vonnie and I shared.

"You two get your britches on and let's get moving; the day's wasting away."

Together the three of us walked to where Pinch Gut creek rushed down the mountain, dropping into cascades every time it came to a place it was too hurried to find a way around. The creek water, filtered through the ancient mountain, was used for everything. Vonnie and I helped fill buckets and carry them back to the fire site, holding the heavy load between us.

Grandma emptied the cotton from the blue-and-white striped mattress tickings and washed them in a kettle of water heated in the back yard, feeding the fire with the old batting and deadwood pine. We threw the pinecones on the fire, watching the flames crackle and snap from orange to blue to green. We wrung the ticks out, Vonnie twisting the sturdy mattress covers in one direction and me in the other, then spreading them over a zigzag wood fence that divided the yard from the rise of the mountain.

There wasn't enough new cotton batting at hand, so while the sun dried the mattress and pillow coverings, we gathered pine needles from the forest floor to fill the pillows, first holding them over the fire to smoke out any bugs. New batting would replace the pine the next time anybody went to the general store in town.

Because we helped some and didn't aggravate her too much

with our usual squabbling, Grandma agreed to let us sleep on a pallet of quilts on one of the picnic tables overlooking the valley, pillows of smoky pine scenting our dreams.

Vonnie elbowed me in the side to wake me up, at the same time shushing me to be quiet. She pointed to the path near the outhouse. Headless in the dark, the long white garb floated silently up the path. Too scared to breathe, we huddled deeper under the quilt. Somebody's dog started howling down in the flats. Hairs on my arms prickled up. The ghostly figure approached slowly, leaning hard on a walking stick, then fell to the ground and began moaning and calling out, but we couldn't make out the words.

While the ghost was down, we ran inside to get Grandma. She grabbed her robe and the iron poker leaning against the fireplace, waking Aunt Annie on the way out. Aunt Annie lit a pine-knot torch from the damped-down embers in the fireplace and came running after Grandma.

The man or ghost, whatever it was, collapsed in a heap on the path.

"Land's sakes, that's Teel!" Grandma said, as Aunt Annie rushed past her.

Aunt Annie fell to her knees next to Uncle Teel, holding her ear against his chest to see if his heart was beating.

She trembled when he started to speak.

"Don't take on so, Annie girl, I'm not dead yet." Uncle Teel managed a weak smile. "Right foolish of me, but I got to thinking I wouldn't have no trouble going down to the privy and back without nary a one of you catching me at it. Pretty near did it. Didn't figure on being mistook for no haint though."

It took some doing, but Aunt Annie and Grandma got Uncle Teel on his feet and back into bed without having to wake Uncle Ed. Aunt Annie tended to him while Grandma made cocoa to help everybody settle down and get back to sleep.

The morning sun hopscotched across the porch and woke us up. Or maybe Grandma did. She was sweeping under the table we were sleeping on. I sat up and rubbed the grit from my eyes.

"Time to start the day," she said. "Remember, early to bed and early to rise makes a man healthy, wealthy, and wise."

"Are we wealthy?" I asked, as I splashed water on my face.

"I swan, you beat all with the questions you come up with."

"Well, you and Grandpa get up real early, and you're always saying that."

"Let me figure on that a minute," she replied. "We have our family and our health, that's the most important. We own our home and land and a good automobile too. There's plenty of food for us and extra to share. We don't owe a dime to a solitary soul unless you count the tithes we owe to God, but we pay those faithful every week. By that way of looking at it, I reckon there's some would say we're wealthy. Now that doesn't mean to say we have idle money, because we don't. Despite that, we live a life of abundance. But don't you be getting yourself uppity about it. The Bible says, *'Pride goeth before destruction, and a haughty spirit before a fall.'*"

I started to say, "Yes ma'am," but she wasn't quite finished.

"For unto whomsoever much is given, of him much shall be required," she continued, "so we're expected to help people who aren't as well off. I like to think we have a gracious plenty. Enough to be thankful, but not prideful. Enough to share with those who are in need. Here's something I hope you'll remember all your life—the gift comes with the giving and not the getting."

"Yes ma'am," I said.

Most Call Me Tolly

We had only been at Uncle Teel's for a few days when Grandma spotted a hive low in a hollow tree near the house, a few bees hovering near the opening. She covered herself in Uncle Teel's canvas hunting pants, put her dress on over them, and added boots, jacket, and long leather work gloves. She cut a square six-inch hole in a pillowcase and stitched in a piece of screening she'd cut from an old door, making a pretty good bee mask. A hunting cap, the kind with ear flaps, went on her head. She looked a fright, but she was ready.

First she piled dead brush around the trunk of the tree, setting it on fire to smoke the bees out. As the smoke died down, she raided the deserted hive, breaking out dripping pieces of the comb and dropping them into a bucket, still leaving some for the bees. Vonnie and I watched from a safe distance.

On the way home Grandma picked up a piece of the comb and sniffed it. "That should be real good honey. It's from purple clover from the smell of it. We'll try it out for breakfast."

I took Uncle Teel a soft scrambled egg and a glass of milk with a generous amount of the honey in it. He had taken to spending much of his day sitting on the porch with Uncle Ed, talking about old times and occasionally chuckling about some tomfoolery or other he and Uncle Teel had been into as boys, but mainly just looking out over the valley, taking solace from the land they both loved.

Grandma sent me and Vonnie to scavenge the untended garden for whatever we could find. There were new potatoes big enough for creaming and plenty of wild onions. Half a dozen rhubarb plants looked healthy, and a ragged row of leaf lettuce promised greens for as long as we needed them. Uncle Ed asked for fried ham and creamed potatoes and wilted lettuce salad for supper. He had things at home to tend to, so he was leaving out at daybreak the next day.

Grandma was to drop him a note and let him know when he was to come for us.

The next morning she made up a sack of leftover ham and biscuits and a jug of water to tide him over on the trip home. After saying his goodbyes to the rest of us, Uncle Ed kissed Uncle Teel on the forehead, got in the car, and drove away, waving an arm out the window until he disappeared around the curve of the mountain.

The man walking up the path was round as a jack-o'-lantern, his faded orange hair streaked with silver. He walked with a limp that caused a lopsided bounce. I was of a mind to split him open right there to see if pumpkin flesh and seeds spilled out.

"Good mornin' to you," he called out, a snaggletooth smile on his face. "Let me interduce myself proper-like. I'm Tolerable Thigpen from down near the flats. Most call me Tolly. I seen Teel had company and wanted to see if I can help you folks. I'm a widderer myself since my missus, Virgie, God rest her, was bit by a serpent and the good Lord took her on to Glory. Still I praise His name. I been plannin' to go to town on Saturday, but ain't no reason I can't go d'rectly if they's anything you're in need of." He was studying Grandma real close.

She handed him some money and a list of what she needed, including the rolls of batting for the mattresses.

"I'll have your tucker and other goods back before suppertime if that would do."

"Thank you kindly, Mr. Thigpen. I'm beholden to you." She watched him hitch-hobble down the road.

"Do you think he's tolerable? How come you didn't call him Tolly?"

I'd doubled up on questions, but she just answered one.

"Oh, I expect he's nice enough, least he seems to be. I can't put my finger on it, but something about that man just don't set quite right. But nice or not, I wouldn't be too quick to make fun if I was you. We've got our own peculiar names. Your great-great-grandpa was called Reckless, although I believe his real name was Rickles or something close to that. He was my grandpa on my mother's side. Died on this very mountain. One day we'll go tend the graves and you'll see where he's buried. Now, you run on and see if you and your sister can fill that egg basket."

The chickens had escaped the henhouse and were scratching a pretty good living from mealybugs and grub worms they pecked from underneath dead leaves and bark. One chicken, blue-black in color, laid blue eggs. Aunt Annie said it was called an Easter egg chicken. Vonnie and I played a game to see who could find the most eggs, and the blue eggs counted double. She won, but not by enough to brag about, although she made a big whoop-de-do about it. We found twenty-three eggs that first day.

Grandma put the eggs in a pan of cold water to test for freshness. Three floated to the top and had to be thrown away. With eggs to spare, she made egg butter, drizzling beaten eggs into hot molasses and stirring like the dickens until the mixture was thick and creamy. Aunt Annie wasn't much of a cook, but she thought she'd give egg butter a try herself when Uncle Teel got to feeling better.

True to his word, Tolerable Thigpen showed up just as we were finishing up our supper of chicken and dumplings, a mess of turnip greens, and custard pie. He'd brought all our supplies, plus a bag of penny candy for me and Vonnie, which we divided, picking the horehound out for Grandma because it was her favorite. Of course, she felt obliged to ask him to eat with us.

"I surely would like to break bread with you good folks, but I've got to git to the house for the milkin'. But you wouldn't have to twist on my arm none to git me to carry home some of whatever you got on the fire that smells so good."

Grandma covered a plate full of warm leftovers with waxed paper, taking it out to him on the porch.

He turned back as he was leaving. "Ma'am, if I ain't being too forward, I'd be right privileged to take you and the little gals to Sunday meetin'. That is, of course, if you'd be of a mind to go."

He said he belonged to a church called the Full Gospel Church of True Believers. Grandma thanked him for the offer, but said she couldn't leave Uncle Teel. He said maybe she'd change her mind when Uncle Teel felt a mite better. She told him she and her husband, Preacher Cales, did missionary work starting churches in the mining towns all around Beckley. Tolerable Thigpen looked disheartened to hear there was a Preacher Cales in Grandma's life.

Truth was, Grandma wasn't about to go off anywhere with Tolerable Thigpen, even if it was to church. No telling what people might think.

Uncle Teel's dog, Pony, came loping out of the woods, the polecat stink on him so strong it scalded my nose. His long fur, matted as the sheep he was born to tend, was camouflaged with leaves and twigs and burrs that attached to his coat as he ran through the brush chasing anything that moved.

After a closer look, Grandma decided she'd best use the sheep shears on him. She left the fur on his legs and head, but the rest got shorn almost bald. Once he'd had a couple of lye soap baths in Pinch Gut Creek, his smell improved considerably.

But I still tried to keep upwind of him.

Grandma and I were putting the sheep shears back in a storage shed near the house when an ear-splitting scream pierced the quiet. I took off to see what Vonnie was hollering about now. She was always pitching a fit about something. I busted out laughing when I saw that Wishbone, the big Rhode Island Red rooster, had her trapped in the outhouse at the end of the path below the house.

She'd already thrown the Sears, Roebuck Catalog Aunt Annie kept in the outhouse at him and missed.

Grandma gave me a look.

I couldn't help it, I'd already got to laughing too hard to quit.

The rooster, cinnamon and black and turquoise feathers all ruffed up, strutted back and forth in front of the door, so pleased with himself he was almost grinning. Every time Vonnie peeked out he charged, launching himself sideways, talons set to strike, all the while letting out a squawk that rivaled the squeals she let out every time he started at her. Now that I'd stopped laughing, the two of them were giving me a headache. If Grandma hadn't been there, I might have left Vonnie to stew for a while.

Howling and whooping, I grabbed the broom off the porch and chased the rooster away while Grandma and Pony herded Vonnie back into the house. Although she was not harmed one bit, Vonnie was still yowling at the sky like there was a new moon. I told her to stop acting like a big bawl-baby. And I will own up to that not helping the situation.

Grandma told me to say I was sorry, and I did, but really I wasn't.

I knew a bawl-baby when I saw one.

Survivors Will Be Shot

We were settling in to the third week at Uncle Teel's house. It was kind of like a vacation, except for him being so sick and all. When Vonnie and I were getting along good, we played jacks on the porch. When we got bored with jacks, we gathered wild teaberries. The little berries, similar to blueberries in size, were reddish pink and grew in clusters on an evergreen plant close to the ground. Teaberries are good to eat, but other than teaberry gum, I didn't know much else they were good for until I saw Grandma pound the leaves with a glass jar and steep them in hot water to make tea. She said the leaves, called wintergreen by some, were known to relieve pains and aches and she thought that would soothe Uncle Teel.

I'd try to remember that the next time Vonnie and old Wishbone gave me a headache.

Vonnie and I discovered a trail that disappeared into the thick of the woods and looped back to join the road, and we'd started walking around the circle every afternoon before supper. Grandma said she felt like getting out of the house a little, so she came with us, and besides, she wanted to see where we were traipsing off to every day.

We didn't see any signs of people most of the way, but there were a couple of houses that looked as if they had grown right up from the dirt, got tired of the struggle, and leaned against the mountain for support. The first house had pink flowers planted in lard cans lined up along the porch railing. Glass bottles hung from every branch of one tree, turning the whole thing into chimes when the breeze came through. Grandma said some thought the bottles caught evil spirits and trapped them inside, but she didn't believe that foolishness. Gourds made into birdhouses were suspended from branches of another tree. The other house was squalid, the air around it heavy with the disappointments of life. A rusted car was propped up on cinder blocks and an old tricycle lay turned over in the dirt. I saw a dingy curtain move as we passed. We heard a dog bark a few times, but we never saw it. Grandma reached down and picked up a good-sized stick just in case.

We heard singing before we could tell where it was coming from. The hymn was "'Tis So Sweet to Trust in Jesus." Grandma thought it might be from a church we could go to while we were there, so we followed the music down an overgrown path to a small building that was not quite a house and not quite a church. The door was closed and no one was around. A sign on a tree nearby warned KEEP AWAY—SURVIVORS WILL BE SHOT, but the door to the building had ALL TRUE BELIEVERS WELCOME painted on it in the same writing.

Grandma decided to believe the sign on the door.

I hoped she was right.

We walked around to the side and peered into a window. Several narrow slats missing from the closed shutters allowed us to view what was going on inside without being seen. A man stood swaying in front of a few rows of benches lining the back wall, an open Bible in one hand and a snake coiled around the other.

The man was Tolerable Thigpen.

I was on the edge of saying something when Grandma pressed her finger to her mouth, motioning me to be quiet.

There were probably ten or twelve people in the room. They came forward one by one as the spirit moved them, reaching deep into the box and bringing forth a snake. Several of the worshipers began to move, shuffling their feet and turning in circles as they let the snakes crawl over their bodies. I looked for fear in their eyes and found none.

A woman handed her baby to the man standing next to her and walked to the front as if in a trance. She stood with arms out-stretched, her face lifted to the heavens in ecstasy. Her hair, so light I could see the blue of her dress through it, came past her waist.

Tolerable Thigpen spoke to her and she dipped her chin in a nod.

He pulled a good-sized copperhead from a bag and draped it around her neck. I thought of the colored picture of Eve and the serpent in Grandpa's Bible. The snake lifted and looked her in the eye. She held the gaze for a heartbeat, then fell into a heap on the floor. Not a soul moved to help her. The snake slithered across her motionless body. All of a sudden the woman began to shake and tremble and roll around. I heard the singing start up again, just one voice this time, high and quivering, shaping the words into prayers and lifting them over the little congregation.

'Tis so sweet to trust in Jesus,
And to take him at his word,
Just to rest upon his promise,
And to know, Thus saith the Lord.
Jesus, Jesus, how I trust him
How I've proved him o'er and o'er.

Jesus, Jesus, precious Jesus
O for grace to trust him more.
I'm so glad I learned to trust him
Precious Jesus, Savior, Friend.
And I know that thou art with me
Will be with me to the end.

The snake coiled next to the makeshift pulpit. A large man, red faced and sweating, reached toward its head to pick it up. The snake's tongue flicked out to taste the smell of its foe before it struck. The man jerked back, stumbling over the box that held the snakes.

I didn't get to see if anybody got bit, because Grandma yanked us away from the window, Vonnie by one hand and me by the other. She was walking so fast my feet only hit the ground every other step.

"Those people are snake handlers. Sometimes they drink poison, strychnine, I've heard tell, and most of them live to tell about it. Better not let me catch you going anywhere near that road again. I wouldn't venture to guess how many snakes got loose around here."

"Yes ma'am," we said.

"Now I mean it," Grandma said, her voice pitched a little higher than usual. "You two stay close to the house because your Uncle Teel's got plenty of property for you to find mischief without going off looking for it. And don't either one of you mention a word of this to your Aunt Annie or anybody else once we get back to the house because a man's religion is his own business as far as I'm concerned and if he wants it told he'll tell it his own self."

"Picking up snakes is about the dumbest thing I ever heard of," I said.

Vonnie spoke up quick and agreed with me, which didn't happen all that often.

"I don't doubt the man is sincere in his beliefs," Grandma said, "but I think God gave us sense enough to leave snakes alone, sense enough not to drink strychnine—or the rubbing alcohol either for that matter. But then, it's not my place to be judging them. The Bible is plain about that. It also says that He who is for me is not against me."

I asked Grandma what would make them think of picking up snakes in the first place.

"The Bible says if you have enough faith, you can pick up serpents and not be harmed, but I don't think God's going to be offended if I don't take Him up on it."

Grandma always knew what God thought.

She and God were on real good terms.

A Handful of
the Mountain

Just as the old rooster crowed the beginning of a new day, Uncle Teel took his last breath on this earth. Grandma said the early morning hours were when a man's life force seemed to ebb at its lowest, but she didn't know why. Uncle Teel, who had been on the mend, had taken a sudden downhill turn. Grandma and Aunt Annie sat with him all night long, moistening his lips with cool mint tea and praying, him not knowing who they were or where he was, fighting them when they tried to cool his brow or straighten his covers.

Grandma and Aunt Annie prepared him for burial. They dressed him in the black suit with the long jacket.

The coffin was a plain pine box, lined with the worn crazy quilt Uncle Teel favored. It was what he wanted. Several stout poles, three, or maybe four, were placed underneath and extended out a couple of feet on each side. Men in overalls, some with a jacket if they had one, and some in full Sunday-go-to-meeting garb, picked the coffin up by the poles and carried it to a grave dug in the family plot right there on Flat Mountain. The men and women, somber in black and brown and navy, stood in silhouette against buckets of rhododendron. Someone had woven flowers through a wreath of wild grapevines and laid it at the head of the grave.

Uncle Teel's name and birthday and deathday were printed on

a piece of paper and placed in a Mason jar, the lid screwed down tight. A man placed the jar at the head of the grave. Some graves had simple wood crosses with the names and dates carved out and a few had real tombstones, but most were marked with the makeshift jars. Other jars held flowers, and one held a picture of a baby that had no name. The traveling preacher was off in the next county, so Tolerable Thigpin, holding an open Bible, stepped from the group of mourners and read from Psalms,

> *"Thou hidest thy face, they are troubled; thou takest away their breath, they die, and return to their dust.*
> *"Thou sendest forth thy spirit, they are created; and thou renewest the face of the earth.*
> *"The glory of the* LORD *shall endure forever; the* LORD *shall rejoice in his works.*
> *"He looketh on the earth, and it trembleth; he toucheth the hills, and they smoke.*
> *"I will sing unto the* LORD *as long as I live; I will sing praise to my God while I have my being.*
> *"My meditation of him shall be sweet; I will be glad in the* LORD.
> *"Let the sinners be consumed out of the earth, and let the wicked be no more. Bless thou the* LORD, *O my soul. Praise ye the* LORD."

Tolerable Thigpen prayed and said, "Amen," and everybody else said, "Amen," then the pallbearers lowered the casket on ropes. While we sang "In the Sweet By and By" and "When the Roll is Called Up Yonder," each mourner walked past and threw a handful of the mountain back into the open grave. Then Tolerable Thigpen rolled up his shirtsleeves to help shovel dirt into the grave, stopping to pay his respects to Grandma and Aunt Annie.

"Teel Adkins wuz a fine fellow. Once he helped me get my cow on her feet when she wuz down. Me and him lumbered all around these parts years past. Like to interduce my eldest, Virginia Thigpen," he said, nodding toward the young woman standing next to him. "She was named Virginia after her sainted mother, who was called Virgie, God rest her, so we called her Ginny. Then she give this baby girl she's holdin' the name Virginia. She's called Nia."

To anybody meeting her that day, Ginny Thigpen would seem like an ordinary person, but I knew better. The last time I saw her, she was wearing a copperhead snake around her neck.

Most of the mourners came back to the house after the funeral. The women brought in food and set it out on the big picnic tables, then busied about picking up plates and washing them under the waterfall in the yard as people finished eating. Men took turns chopping logs into firewood to replenish the stack of kindling on the porch. From time to time they passed a pint jar of moonshine, turning their backs so the women on the porch could pretend they didn't notice.

Grownups with death clouding their eyes talked about life while children laughed and played in the yard. Vonnie and I joined in endless rounds of Red Rover and Ring Around the Rosie. After that, someone started a game of Hide and Seek. From my hiding place high in the saddle fork of a maple tree, I could see people gathered on the porch. The big picnic tables were filled and over-flowing. I thought Uncle Teel would be pleased. Grandma said he always did like a lot of company.

Aunt Annie had too nervous a disposition to stay alone where Uncle Teel died, so she went to stay with relatives in another county, leaving us to close up the house.

Tolerable Thigpen sent Ginny to help us. Vonnie and I played with baby Nia, making her a sugar tit from a spoonful of sugar tied up in a piece of cloth and taking her for rides in the wheel-barrow. We scattered corn to bait the coop so Grandma could catch a chicken most any time she wanted. One whole day she lured the chickens in one by one and wrung their necks. She chopped the heads off, watching as they ran around spurting blood from headless bodies. After they fell over dead, she dipped them in boiling water, plucked the feathers, lit a pine knot torch to singe the pinfeathers, then gutted and cut them up.

Turkey vultures held watch from a dead pine tree, lifting grotesque bodies to rearrange their wings from time to time.

After Grandma boiled the chickens in the big outdoor kettle, she added a handful of salt, boned the meat, and packed it in mason jars, pouring broth to an inch from the top. She had Ginny wipe the rims of the jars with cider vinegar to cut any grease so the lids would seal properly in the big canner. There were fourteen chickens put up and ready to use for chicken and dumplings. Grandma sent four of the jars home with Ginny.

Tolerable Thigpen stopped by to say he was right sorry to see us go. Grandma asked him to keep an eye on the place since Aunt Annie was figuring to come back to Flat Mountain in the spring. He perked up at that. Grandma gave him the stack of newly cut firewood from the porch, and he took Pony home with him.

I sat on the porch and watched him walk away, dipping to one side with each step.

The vultures settled to the ground and picked at the guts and bones and the bloodied dirt until no trace of death remained.

Lead a Horse to Water

The house felt strange when we got home from Flat Mountain. Like being in a cemetery, where the air was always flat as a flitter. I'd heard it said you couldn't fly a kite in a cemetery even on a windy day because the air didn't have any lift to it. I'd never tried it though. Although Grandpa had been home all along, a house needed more than one person to give it life so as there could be a give and take, at least according to Grandma, and the more people in it, the more life there was. It must have been true because something important had left our house while we were gone, and we'd have to laugh and cry and pray and fuss and work inside those rooms to get it back.

Grandma thought Grandpa was looking a little peaked, but she reckoned all he needed was a few biscuits and gravy to give him some color. Nobody talked about Uncle Teel dying, not a single word. It seems like we would have, but we didn't. That's just how we were. Grandma made a big supper and kept putting more on Grandpa's plate until he finally told her he was up to his eyeballs and couldn't eat another bite and besides, it was time to get ready for prayer meeting if she was really set on going. She was.

A few trees concealed a stone-circled fire site that had seen too many butts and not enough fires. Most everybody called it the ash pit, but I'd heard some call it the arm pit. The odor of stamped-out cigarettes and unrepented sins soured the air.

Roby Stover made a beeline there as soon as he could escape the Wednesday night prayer meeting for a couple of minutes. I didn't know why we called him Roby when everybody else was called Brother This or Sister That. Grandma would know, but I wasn't so sure she'd tell me. There was a lot of stuff she said wouldn't hurt me one iota not to know.

While everybody shook hands with the people around them, even those they'd seen earlier at the post office or the Piggly Wiggly, Roby ducked back in. He wasn't fooling me. A person needn't smell the Sen-Sen on him to know that he'd been sneaking a smoke. Sen-Sen was a licorice candy advertised as "breath perfume." Most of the men at the ash pit carried a packet of it tucked away. But Sen-Sen did little to cover the lingering smell of the Chesterfield or Lucky Strike or Camel cigarettes they tried to keep secret from meddling wives and girlfriends.

My grandpa preached hard as any man could against smoking and drinking. He said Roby hadn't quit his sinful ways because the Holy Ghost hadn't convicted him yet. When he got convicted, he'd lay those poisons down and never be tempted to pick them up again. It hadn't happened yet, but Grandpa had faith it would. In the meantime he'd keep praying for Roby to be delivered. That was all a man could do. God would do the rest. Grandpa was sure of it.

"You can lead a horse to water," he said, shaking his head, "but you can't make him drink."

I wasn't sure what that meant, so I just nodded.

Grandma and Grandpa were talking about how Roby Stover had been sorrier than a hound dog before he took up with Roberta Crawford. Roby's real name was Roberts, like there was more than one of him, but I'd never heard him called that. It was funny how their first names matched up—Roberts and Roberta. They even favored some. Both were tall and rangy. And both of them had thin hair, except Roby's was reddish and Roberta's a dirty blonde. Dishwater blonde, Grandma called it.

"Roberta's not much on looks," Grandma said.

Grandpa said that was being downright generous. He'd heard one of the men say if that girl's face got any longer they'd have to put a feedbag on her.

Grandma started to laugh, then caught herself. "That's a terrible thing to say about a nice girl like Roberta. She's smart too. Graduated high school and is in the college downtown studying stenography. I wouldn't have thought she would have the likes of Roby on a buttered biscuit. Now they're married and she's got him coming to services regular. There's not a one among us who thought that would come to be."

Grandpa said he was wrong to have repeated that talk about Roberta.

"I'm as much to blame as you are," Grandma said, "but neither of us spoke anything that wasn't the truth."

Grandpa put a serious look on. "Speaking in jest is a mighty poor excuse for being unkind. We best seek the Lord's forgiveness for acting the fool."

According to Grandpa and Grandma, eavesdropping and gossiping were sins just the same as stealing and lying and wearing feathers. If you eavesdropped, you stole things that weren't meant for your ears, and if you gossiped, you could besmirch a person's good name. As for wearing feathers, all I knew was it said not to in The Rules. My mother wore a hat with feathers and no harm came, but she wasn't a Pentecostal. I hadn't worn any feathers unless the one I wore as Hiawatha for a program at school counted.

But I *had* eavesdropped and gossiped.

And I was fixing to do it again.

I could not wait to tell Sissy every word. I rehearsed it in my head, toying with the idea of whinnying when I got to the part about putting the feedbag on Roberta.

The church was dark when we arrived for the Sunday evening service. Grandma cut on the lights and started down the pews straightening hymnals, while I looked for the fan with the picture of a blue-eyed Jesus. Paper fans always stood ready in the wooden rack on the back of each pew, along with the hymnals. Each fan was the size of a small paper plate and had a flat stick attached as a handle. Sometimes you got a fan with a picture of Jesus on one side and Scripture verses on the other, while another time your fan might advertise a bank or a furniture store.

At the last meeting Sister Persinger got to the Jesus fan first and I'd had to ask her to trade, which made me uneasy because that woman had a snurl on her face all the time. She didn't like children all that much, and she clearly harbored a particular dislike for me. It could have to do with me catching her in the vestibule pinching her cheeks all rosy before she went wringing and twisting down the aisle to sit next to Clive Farleigh, one of the few available men we had.

I looked her square in the eye.

Her lips pursed up like she had a drawstring around her mouth, but she handed me the fan before Grandma was any the wiser. Roby came in and slouched down next to Roberta, who had arrived early with some neighbors. She said something to him, and he took off his jacket and draped it over her shoulders. The rest of the congregation arrived in twos and threes, until there were people scattered on most of the pews, though not as many as at the morning service.

Grandpa said most wanted their salvation served up in small portions.

"You might take that into consideration Sunday morning when I've got dinner drying out in the oven," Grandma said.

"The Lord leads me, Rindy. I am but a lowly servant doing His will."

"I don't expect His will is for me to serve up a stringy roast for Sunday dinner."

"I've been eating your cooking since you were but a girl of eighteen and haven't felt compelled to complain yet," Grandpa said.

"It wouldn't do you to, even if you did feel the need." Grandma turned back to straightening hymnals.

The opening hymn was sung by Sister Singletary. She was the only one up to doing a solo since we'd lost Brother Bennett to the Nazarenes. After that, Grandpa made some announcements: The roof had sprung a leak and he'd need a volunteer to help him tar it before the next rain caught them unawares. The Ladies Home Missionary Society was organizing a prayer chain for the missionaries overseas. The 7:00 p.m. Thursday men's Bible study was starting back up again. Sunday next was Valentine's Day, so the preaching would be on God's love, the greatest love of all. "Now for all you fellows out there, remember to get your sweetheart a valentine or a box of chocolates," he'd added.

Then Grandpa called for testimonies. A testimony was when someone got up and said what a terrible person he had been until he got saved.

"Why don't the women get up and tell the bad things they've done?" I asked Grandma.

"It's not seemly for women to put themselves forward. Besides," she continued, "the women aren't as sinful as the men, at least by my thinking. Not a one comes to mind that smokes or drinks or gambles. Now the women do sin, each and every one of us does, but our sins are things like backbiting or being covetous or stingy or vain. Folks don't get themselves as worked up about those sins, but I reckon they should. Women," she said, "are held to a higher standard. Men are a different story."

Each one of the testimony-giving men had been the worst drunkard or the biggest liar or most lowdown cheater or gambler

or some combination of all those things, that is, of course, until
he got saved. Their stories were well-rehearsed from repeated
tellings, and most of us pretty well knew what came next.

Some of the men never felt called to testify. Maybe it was
because they didn't want to disappoint the folks who'd expect
them to confess to the same awful sins the drunkards owned up
to, puffing their chests as they got to the worst parts. The men
who didn't testify looked hangdog to me, like they were ashamed
they didn't have sins bad enough to brag about.

Grandma said some in the church believed Roby had no
business testifying because he wasn't saved.

I asked why everybody called him by his first name.

"Same reason. It's because he hasn't got saved and joined the
church family. If he was older, we'd call him Mister Stover, but
he's hardly more than a boy and folks have known him all his
life, so we'd have trouble with the Mister. I expect he would too.
Irregardless, we're glad Roby and Roberta are worshiping with us
regular. All are welcome and equal here, saints and sinners alike."

I didn't know much about saints, but I did know that Roby
was a big sinner. Maybe the biggest one I'd heard testify.

Grandma wondered if Roby might be getting a mite too fond
of standing up and repeating the same old story over and over.

Grandpa said it wasn't for him to chastise anyone for speaking out in the house of the Lord.

As he sometimes did when he got up to testify, Roby added
on a sin we hadn't heard before, something about doing his saint-
of-a-wife wrong. I didn't know what he had done, but I could tell
it was bad from the sheepish look on his face. He said he couldn't
say more because the innocent children and womenfolk there
didn't need to hear such talk, but surely everybody knew what he
meant.

I didn't.

Whatever it was that Roby confessed to caused heads to wag
and whispers to hiss up and down the scarred wooden pews.

When I asked Grandma, she said I didn't need to be worrying myself about Roby Stover's sins, just to worry about my own.

She stood there looking at me until I remembered.

"Yes ma'am," I said.

I was a little anxious about that look. I hoped she didn't know about the times Sissy and I played gin rummy all night. That was the only sin I could think of that might send me straight to Hell. I wondered if Sissy would go to Hell too but decided she wouldn't. She was a Methodist, and they didn't care one way or the other if you gambled all night. No matter how I ran it around in my head, I couldn't make it come out fair that I'd go to Hell and she wouldn't for the very same sin. It came to me then that some things never would be fair. I'd decided to be a Methodist when I grew up. So I hoped God would remember that and take it into account.

Grandpa preached a whole flock of angels down from Heaven that night. Despite his best efforts, it looked like nobody was coming forward to get saved.

But Grandpa wasn't one to give up easy.

"Let's sing the first and last verse one more time," he said for the third time. "The Lord is reaching out to you tonight, ready to cleanse you of your sins for all eternity. If you are tired, He'll be your resting place. If you are disappointed, He'll be your hope for tomorrow. If you are lonely, He'll be your faithful companion. He's calling for you to come home."

The congregation, heads bowed, sang, "Come home, come home, ye who are weary come home . . ."

Roby lurched up from his seat and began to shout, "Praise the Lord!" and "Hallelujah!" with tears flying off his face and splotching his blue chambray work shirt. Grandpa continued with the invitation and others sang, while still others started praying and speaking in tongues. Grandma went down on her knees and began to utter words I couldn't make sense of. Every line and wrinkle dissolved from her face. Lit from within, her gaze transfixed by sights unseen by me, she repeated the words again and again, her voice soft and urgent.

Next thing I knew, Roby was on his knees, head held in his hands, praying like his life depended on it. Even though he was a sinner, Roby Stover was one of the best we had at praying. Grandpa went back and knelt by his side, his right arm around Roby's shoulder, beseeching him to come forward and give his life to the Lord.

As the last of the chorus was sung and nobody answered the call, Grandpa strode to the front and lifted his arms to give the benediction.

Afterwards, the men and women broke into separate clusters in the churchyard. Grandma huddled with Sister Wood and some others from the Home Missionary Society. I waited nearby, straining to hear every word the women said.

"Must have taken her better than a week to make that dress."

"Outlandish for a married woman, if you want my opinion."

"Beaver's Grocery is carrying notions. But land's sake, they'll put you in the poor house."

"I heard tell Jayboy, he's her youngest, is home on furlough from the Navy."

"You don't reckon he'll go sniffing around that Jones girl again?"

"He won't if her daddy catches wind of it."

Roby's name wasn't even mentioned. The women had witnessed his tearful confessions before and were sure to again. Besides, they had newer things to gossip about.

As Roby put Roberta in the neighbor's car, he gave her a quick pat on the behind.

Sister Wood's eyebrows shot up. Before she could sputter a single word of rebuke, Roby turned tail and swaggered off in the direction of the ash pit.

On the way home Grandma said it was such a pity Roby didn't get saved.

"Yes," Grandpa said, "but I've got a feeling the Lord's going to win the battle next time. Sure as the world, I do believe it. Do I hear an amen?"

"Amen," me and Grandma said.

A Gizzard on My Fork

Sometimes the Pentecostals held a revival meeting in a tent that looked big enough to hold the circus that came to town every year. Ragtag boys from the neighborhood hoped to earn pocket change for setting up rows of mismatched fold-up chairs. A big sign across the makeshift stage declared JESUS SAVES, and the evangelist preaching might be a little bit famous in Pentecostal circles.

Side flaps of the tent were folded up so you could hold to the hope a whiff of breeze would find its way through the crowded rows to where you were sitting. A chorus of preaching and praying and shouting and singing blurred into the night. The hymn "Just as I Am" flowed over bowed heads as the service came to a close.

Moths as big as baby birds flocked around the lights.

We kept the good bedroom, the downstairs one with a small sitting room attached, for visiting missionaries and preachers, the rest of us crowding upstairs into three low-ceilinged attic bedrooms. The little-bit-famous preacher came home with us from the evening service. Grandma heated up the blackberry cobbler and whipped up a whole mixing bowl of fresh cream.

The preacher patted his mouth with a napkin made from a white flour sack.

"Sister Cales, I have been privileged to dine in some of the finest cafés and eateries in Franklin County, and I have not to this day been served anything of an equal to your blackberry cobbler."

Grandma thought that was worth another helping. The pie,

spooned up in flat soup bowls with a generous heap of the cream on top, washed down easy with big glasses of sweet milk.

And that put everyone to sleep in no time.

Missionaries who always seemed to be just back from Africa stayed with us. Sister Guyandott lived with us all summer one time. She wanted the church to send her supplies packed in popcorn to share with the natives who didn't know about civilized treats like exploding corn. She also wanted a supply of unpopped corn so she could demonstrate the magic of it when she got back to Africa. I thought she wanted to scare the natives right out of their pagan beliefs into being good Pentecostals and covering up their naked bodies from necks to ankles and elbows and never again painting their faces or wearing beads around their necks or feathers on their heads.

After the closing service, the Pentecostals held a dinner on the ground. A picnic could be held by anyone, but dinner on the ground was different—only the church held dinner on the ground. Food was pulled from baskets and boxes and paper bags and set out on sawhorse tables made with planks and covered with extra sheets the women had brought. If I squinted my eyes against the sun, the circle of quilts spread on the ground turned into a kaleidoscope of fanciful designs. Folks sitting down to eat their dinners and catch up on the news gradually blotted out the colorful shapes.

"Brother Harvey, you got any Elsie's pups left? Like to have one for my boy if you do."

"Sister Sutphin, how's your girl over in Charleston doing?"

"James Junior, you get your feet off that quilt before I come over there."

"Be sure to get a piece of Sister Wood's fried chicken. She soaks it in buttermilk, you know."

Their voices had the twang of the mountains, like a softly strummed banjo gone a little off tune.

There were whole hams and fried chickens and meatloaves, baked beans and cabbage slaw and deviled eggs, pickled eggs and pickled green beans and homemade sour pickles that turned your mouth inside out before they ever touched your tongue, biscuits and cornbread and loaves of light bread from the store. The men without wives brought the store-bought bread.

"That stuff's not fit to eat," Grandma said with a little sniff, but she put a piece on her plate when she thought I wouldn't notice. I wanted her to stay in a good mood, so I didn't let on.

Sister Wood's platter of fried chicken was disappearing fast. Grandma said for me to hurry on over there and get a piece. I sure hoped I could find me a gizzard. Sister Harper saw me poking through the chicken and said, "Honey, I brought them pickled beans you like so much. You go get you some."

"Yes ma'am," I said, coming up with a gizzard on my fork.

The flat pan of macaroni and cheese Sister Blankenship served up looked just like Grandma's. When I mentioned it, she laughed. "Well, it ought to. I'm the one told her how to go about fixing it." I put some on my plate. Still, I made sure to save a little room for Grandma's cake. I remembered to tell her I didn't think Sister Blankenship's macaroni was quite as good as hers. She said, "I swan, you are a sight." But her eyes told me she liked the compliment.

I wandered over to find me a spot. The Drunkard's Path was my favorite quilt pattern, but I guess Grandma thought it wasn't fitting for a church social, so she'd brought a quilt called Jacob's Ladder. She was busy talking to Sister Wood. I stopped to listen and caught the tail end of something about that last one being the image of his best friend. I was hoping to have more to tell Sissy, but I couldn't make out much of what they were saying. I sidled my way closer.

Grandma gave me a look.

I scooted out of there to get me a piece of cake.

Desserts of all kinds and colors made accidental centerpieces on the tables. There were rhubarb, cherry, and apple crumb pies worthy of blue ribbons. An angel food cake piled with strawberries, another cake stiff with walnuts, and a vanilla cake with boiled frosting all vied for attention.

But Grandma's cake was best.

She made an Appalachian stack cake with lots of thin molasses-flavored layers put together with homemade cinnamon apple butter. She said the cake was sad, but that didn't have anything to do with being down in the dumps, it was just our way of saying it was moist and heavy. She told me that stack cake was used for weddings and funerals and other socials back when she was a girl. Baking was costly, so each woman brought a layer to add to the cake or a jar of apple butter or cherry preserves to smear between the layers.

Brother Dub called for me to bring him some of Grandma's cake. His last name was Williams, but everybody always just called him Brother Dub. Grandma said the Dub probably came from the first letter of his last name. He only had one leg so it was kind of hard for him to get around. Grandma said he'd got his leg blown off in the War and that was a shame. I cut an extra big piece and walked it over to him, balancing it on two slightly greasy hands.

By way of thanks he said it looked like I just might grow up to be as fine of a woman as my grandma.

I didn't have the heart to tell him he was wrong about how I was going to turn out. After all, he had no way of knowing about me and Sissy gambling with real cards all night.

Finally everyone picked up their dishes and quilts and, like a scene played backwards, everything went back into baskets and boxes and paper bags.

It had been a grand day.

A shooting star silvered through the dusky sky. I stopped and closed my eyes to make a wish. I wished for my mother to come home.

Grandma said if I didn't stop being such a slowpoke we never would get home.

"Yes ma'am," I said.

Suffer the Little Children

Like a tribe worshiping a false idol, we sat bowed around the big Philco radio in the front room, leaning forward not to miss a single word Rochester said about Jack Benny and his cheapskate ways. My brother, Hursey, home from Romney School for the Deaf, came busting in, raring to tell Grandma something or other. Although I motioned him to wait, it was too late—we'd missed the funny part. It was done without giving it a thought—that hand I held up to stop Hursey from interrupting, but there was a look came over his face I'd never noticed before, maybe because I wasn't much interested in anything that didn't have me in the center of it. Yet the hurt I sensed come over my brother at that moment came over me as well.

Hursey Clev, feisty and sharp as a tack, was the spitting image of our daddy, whose given name he carried, and the Clev, of course, he got from Grandpa Luther Clevland Cales. My mother was only sixteen when she had him, just a child herself, my daddy twenty-three. They'd run off and got married when she was fifteen, but it was too late for Grandpa to do much about it besides shooting my daddy with his double-barreled shotgun.

Grandma said the thought likely crossed his mind.

A smile twitching at her mouth, she shook her head. "Oh he was a charmer, your daddy was, coming around with silver-blond hair and a silver tongue. The way he set his sights on your mother, there was no stopping him. Your mother was shy as a girl, but willful too. Some are at that age, as I expect you'll find out when you have young'uns of your own. The apple doesn't fall far from the tree."

"I don't want any babies when I grow up," I told her.

"You're likely to change your mind when you get a little farther down the road," she said.

"Nope, not a one," I repeated.

Dangling a soggy baby on my hip all day didn't interest me one bit. I had in mind to ride an elephant through the jungle with a parrot named Echo on my shoulder and sing songs we both knew all the words to, like "Zippity Doo Dah" and "You Are My Sunshine."

Grandma told me the story about when my brother was little and got very sick. She said it wasn't like him not to be outside running and playing with the other children who lived nearby. But one day he took to laying around, all the energy sucked out of him. Then he started complaining of a headache and felt warm. By suppertime he was burning with a fever that cold rags didn't do a thing to bring down. Next day he was vomiting and said his neck hurt, so the company doctor in Lynwynn, that's the coal camp where they were living at the time, was sent for. But first he had to deliver Marlene Mae Haegar's baby up in Yell Again Holler. Marlene was having some trouble so the doctor couldn't say when, but he promised to come when he could.

A holler was the small valley between the folds of two mountains. Yell Again Holler got its name because it was so narrow ever little noise carried so far that if you wanted someone who lived along the flats, you just stood at the bottom and yelled the name of who you wanted to come down to meet you. You were sure to be heard by the first house, they'd yell again to the next, and so on, until word got to the right person.

After Marlene suffered hours of tears and travail, the doctor delivered a boy, a blue baby who never took his first breath. She was bleeding bad, so he'd had to tend to her, the baby dark and lifeless in her arms, before he could start for our house.

Noon came and went before the doctor finally got there, Marlene Mae Haegar's blood still wet on his clothes. Grandma heated a basin of water and sliced off a piece of lye soap so he could wash up before he looked down Hursey's throat and in his ears and up his nose and listened to the gurgles of his stomach and the beatings of his heart, prodding and poking at his little boy body. She remembered a streak on the doctor's forehead where he'd pushed his hair aside with a bloody hand when he was tending Marlene. Funny how some little thing like that will stick in your mind.

Grandma had stewed an old rooster until the meat on his bones fell off, thickened up the broth, and pinched off biscuit dough to make the kind of puffy dumplings Hursey liked. Still, he only ate a bite or two. The doctor was another story. He hadn't eaten a hot meal since the day before, so he made up for it by downing a big portion of that rooster along with generous helpings from the pot of leather britches, potatoes, and onions jiggling together in a savory broth. Leather britches were green beans threaded onto strings and hung from the ceiling to dry, which toughened up the shells. If you wanted a mess ready for supper, you had best put them on the fire before you measured out the coffee for breakfast.

He sure did hate to eat and run, but it couldn't be helped, the doctor had said, pulling off the napkin he'd tucked under his collar to protect his stained green necktie. He said there's a baby over toward the tipple waiting to be born and he prayed to God that little one would have a better outcome than the one he just came from. He told Grandma to try to get some broth down Hursey and to keep on with the wet rags. Other than that, there was little else to be done.

All that time he was talking to Grandma, looking right past my mother.

Being ignored like that did not set well with her. When the doctor picked up his black valise to leave, Grandma said my mother reared right up on her hind legs and told the doctor this was her child, and she knew a place where something else could be done. She had driven a car since she was fourteen years old, so she'd picked Hursey up then and there and carried him out, all swaddled in a quilt, and laid him on the backseat.

My daddy and Grandpa were both down in the mines, Grandma said, and there was no way to get word to them, so my mother drove through a snow storm to the hospital in Beckley, leaving Grandma to tend to Vonnie, her still a babe in arms. A man saw her struggling up the icy hospital steps, Hursey heavy in her arms, and took him from her and carried him inside. The man smelled of antiseptic and another odor she couldn't name, camphor maybe, and when she followed him through the double doors those same odors, stronger still and mixed with bleach, sickened her stomach. She swallowed hard to quell the urge to retch. When she saw a Christmas tree in the corner of the room, she realized it was the pine sap she smelled. Unable to think of Christmas, now only days away, she turned her back on the tree and its hateful red and green lights.

The overheated waiting room steamed with faceless people in woolen sweaters and scarves and coats that gave off the odor of wet dogs. They hadn't made her wait in that room though, and she was grateful to the man for that. Turned out he was the first of many doctors brought in to shake their heads over this child who was sick unto death.

The doctor ordered the nurses to strip Hursey and put him in and out of an ice bath until they got his temperature down. Over the next day or two they put him through every test they knew to do. Mother told her the worst were the spinal taps, holding him down while they stabbed long needles into his back that made him scream like an animal. And the next day they did it again. Finally the big-shot doctors, who were pretty near as useless as the company doctor from home, least by her way of thinking, came up with a name for what my brother had.

Spinal meningitis.

It was a relief in a way to put a name to the enemy they were fighting.

But Grandma said that was before my mother knew exactly what it was they were dealing with. The doctor who carried Hursey into the hospital explained that spinal meningitis was an infection caused by bacteria that somehow got into the bloodstream and settled in the spinal cord and the brain. He was trying a course of sulfa drugs, but she should know she had a very sick boy. It was a fearsome battle ahead, and make no mistake, this disease could kill him.

If Hursey had only got the spinal meningitis a few years later, they might have given him penicillin shots, and that would have cured him before the disease took its hold. But it was 1937 that he got sick. It wasn't until 1944 that a patient at Fairmont General Hospital in West Virginia became the first person ever to be treated with a full course of penicillin. Fairmont was only a Sunday drive from Beckley. But for seven years plus the few hours it took to drive there, our brother might not have lost his hearing.

Grandma said everybody was praying God would perform a miracle, and several went with Grandpa to the hospital and laid on hands and prayed that Hursey be delivered from the sickness that had him in its grip, but it wasn't to be.

At least not yet.

Days passed with him in that bed, his head bent back and neck rigid, the slightest movement causing him to cry out in pain. Unable to take more than a few sips of water laced with a little sugar and salt, his baby fat fell off, and muscle too, leaving only the skin and bones of him, at first feverish and convulsing, then pale and still.

But Grandma said Hursey was a fighter.

And she gave God the glory for that, for giving Hursey that fighting spirit.

No matter how many times He let her down, Grandma could always find something good to say about God.

Grandma said the doctors came and stood over Hursey's bed, defeat showing in the slump of their shoulders as they walked away, not knowing whether he'd pull through another night. Yet pull through he did. After a few weeks, he began to improve. His eyes stayed open longer. And he was able to eat a little. Bananas and custard and melted ice cream began to fill out the hollows of his face. Soon he could sit up in bed, then in a chair. Before long he was walking around the halls. Finally the day came he got to go home and be the child he was meant to be, playing in the yard and getting dirty like little boys will.

Grandma said the good Lord had answered their prayers.

When our mother called him for supper one day, he never even looked up. She walked to where he sat holding a wooden car his daddy had made him for Christmas, which they'd put off celebrating until he got home. "Hursey Clev, come on and eat before it gets cold," she'd said to him, thinking he was caught up in some little boy daydream of snips and snails and puppy dog tails. But when he still didn't take notice, she reached down and touched his blond head.

It startled him, and he looked up.

I imagined my brother watching Mother's mouth form shapes that floated toward him and dissolved into thin air without making a sound.

And Mother would have felt the words he breathed out tremble her eardrums and make waves in her head until she finally allowed herself forced herself willed herself to hear what he was telling her plain as day.

"Mommy, I can't hear you."

He was five years old.

I didn't understand why, despite all the prayers of people of unbounded faith, God went against His word and turned a blind eye on my brother.

And I told Grandma so.

"Not thy will, but Mine be done," Grandma reminded me, like she'd heard Him say it yesterday.

I wondered why healing my brother wouldn't be God's will. From what I knew, Hursey hadn't acted near as bad as me. Maybe I'd turn up deaf, or worse.

Grandma told me nothing bad was going to happen to me, so to quit talking foolish. As for why God hadn't healed Hursey, she said it wasn't for us to question why. One day He would reveal His plan in all its glory and we'd understand clear as could be.

No matter how many promises He broke, Grandma never got mad at God.

Over the next several years, doctors, specialists in hearing, tested my brother and fitted him with hearing aids, bulky black boxes that strapped to his chest with ugly wires running to earpieces that hurt his tender ears and didn't help him hear even the loudest sound. He was stone deaf and no hearing aid would ever help. But they sold the useless things to my mother anyway, one after the other, always a newer better one, and for high prices. Of course, it was really hope she was paying for, and sometimes hope comes in a black box with a high price.

One day Hursey ripped his earpieces out and sent the newest ugly box, wires flailing from it like tentacles, into our backyard fishpond to drown under the water lilies. He refused to wear hearing aids again or to listen to anybody who tried to get him to. And if my brother didn't want to listen, he had the perfect solution.

He closed his eyes.

The Flesh Is Weak

We were waiting for God to perform a miracle.
And Merle Hobart was waiting to help Him.

Merle Hobart pulled a handkerchief from his back pocket and dabbed at the sweat on his brow as two middle-aged men, turned so much alike I believed they were twins, separated from the front of the prayer line and made their way across the stage to where he stood in a golden circle of light. Both told him they were afflicted with a lifelong weakness for alcohol. Merle Hobart, white shirt-sleeves rolled halfway up his forearms, reached out and placed a hand on each brother's head.

"Get thee out, Satan! In the name of Jesus, I command you!"

His voice was strong, with more than a hint of backwoods in it. It was a voice easy to believe.

Slain in the spirit, the men fell back and were caught and lowered to the floor by Merle Hobart's disciples. After the brothers regained their senses, they kneeled at his feet, his light reflected on their faces.

"Listen, for I am speaking to you. No, the *Lord* is speaking to you through me. He asked me to tell you He is healing you of the craving for alcohol this very minute. Demons are leaving your body as I'm talking to you. Jesus is filling you up now. I felt the power of His blood surge through my arms like a bolt!"

The men rose to their feet and stumbled off the stage, sobs contorting their faces.

Looking up to Heaven, Merle Hobart prayed, "Thank You, Jesus. Amen and amen."

Words of praise floated up from the crowd:

"Hallelujah!"

"Thank you, Jesus!"

"Praise God!"

Every day at two o'clock Grandma sewed buttons and turned collars and darned socks while she listened to Merle Hobart on the radio. He was a young preacher just starting to make a name for himself, and like my grandma and grandpa, he was in the Pentecostal Holiness Church. Grandma and Grandpa had a lot of faith in God and a good bit in Merle Hobart, so when he announced he was holding a healing meeting hardly more than a day's drive from home, they decided to take my brother to be prayed for, although they had to talk him into it.

Hursey was twelve. I was five and wanted to stick my behind in the backseat every time the car left the driveway, so I begged until Grandma agreed to let me tag along. Since Vonnie, two years older, was in school, Grandma asked Sister Wood to stay with her for the one night we'd be gone. We packed up fried chicken and biscuits and hardboiled eggs and apples and headed out—Grandpa driving, Grandma telling him how to, and me and Hursey already squabbling in the backseat.

It was late when we got to where the meeting was being held, so we found a room in a tourist home to spend the night and rest up for the healing service the next day.

The line of sick people coiled itself like a wounded serpent around the innards of the tent. The man in front of me, so frail I could count his rib bones under his shirt, lay stretched out on a narrow table with wheels, his body tied on with lengths of clothesline. A little girl, withered leg dangling, slept in her daddy's arms, and behind her a young man dragged himself along on homemade crutches.

We never seemed to get closer, although we must have, because the sick and infirm snailed across the stage in a sluggish trail of suffering, littering the floor with crutches and canes and tears offered up in the ecstasy of the healing power of God. I kept wanting to witness a healing I could see, like somebody growing back a missing arm or leg right there in front of me, but not a soul did, even though there was a bunch could have used one.

To pass the time, Hursey and I played a game where he'd draw one of the sick people and I had to guess which one it was, until Grandma saw what we were doing and put a stop to it. After that we played I Spy and Twenty Questions. We couldn't talk out loud so we used sign language to spell everything out, holding our hands low so we wouldn't call unnecessary attention to ourselves. Grandma was dead set against calling attention. She frowned a little and started to say something but decided to leave well enough alone.

A woman with frizzly red hair wheeled herself across the stage. Paralyzed since she fell down her cellar stairs, she said she'd lost all feeling in her legs and couldn't walk a step.

"Rise! Rise up and walk in the name of Jesus!"

The woman pushed up from her wheelchair and took a step toward the flock gathered together in the name of God and Merle Hobart. She started out, her steps halting at first, then speeding up as she trotted back and forth across the stage, shouting and raising her arms in jubilation.

Again, Merle Hobart turned his eyes toward Heaven and prayed. "Thank you, Jesus. Amen and amen."

"Praise the Lord! You won't be needing that old wheelchair anymore. Jesus is standing next to you right now. I can see you leaning on His everlasting arms."

Merle Hobart gave a nod to the choir and they commenced to sing "Leaning on the Everlasting Arms."

I worried God might not bless Hursey with His favor because

I was there, tainting Grandpa and Grandma's goodness. Grandpa had caught me lying more than once, so I was sure God knew all about me. It wouldn't be fair for Him to take my sins out on Hursey, but I'd suspected that God wasn't always fair from other dealings I'd had with him. Still, I didn't want to be too hard to get along with. All He needed to get back in with me was to heal my brother. And if He was in the mood, maybe He'd go right down the line and heal everybody else that needed it.

People suffering with headaches and toothaches and bellyaches and every other ache you could think of were prayed for, and we were still nowhere near the front. When I realized we weren't going to get close enough for Merle Hobart and God to heal Hursey, all I wanted was to go home and wash the film of sickness and sorrow off me, have a supper of fried eggs and sliced tomatoes, and climb in my own bed under Grandma's homemade quilts.

But Grandma and Grandpa kept hoping until the last song was sung and the last prayer was prayed. Grandpa's shoulders, already stooped from working low coal in mines under the West Virginia hills, bent a little lower, and Grandma had that set look on her face, which meant she didn't want to talk about it, and she didn't want to hear anybody else talk about it either. We went back to the tourist home to gather our things and get ready for the long drive home.

"You go wash up, but don't you be getting in that bathtub. Looks clean enough, but there's no telling who's been there before you," Grandma said, filling the sink with hot water and handing me a washrag and a new bar of Ivory soap she'd brought from home.

"Wash down far as Possible, wash up far as Possible, then wash Possible."

Grandma usually grinned at me when she said that, but there was no grin left in her.

We packed up and followed our dim headlights away from Journey's End Tourist Home.

I asked Grandpa why God needed Merle Hobart to help Him heal those people. Grandpa said everything is part of God's master plan, and like the hymn said, we'd understand it all by and by. It seemed to me it was a piss-poor plan. I'd recently heard somebody say piss-poor, and ever since I'd been dying to say it out loud, but of course I didn't dare.

Down the road apiece, we stopped to get us a slice of pie and a cup of black coffee for Grandpa. Hursey was the one that spotted him sitting next to a woman in the back booth of the diner and elbowed Grandpa, who nudged Grandma to look.

"Why, that's Merle Hobart," Grandma said.

I could tell something didn't set too well with her.

Merle Hobart brushed a stray lock of the woman's hair back from her face, his wedding band glinting under the fluorescent tube. I didn't recognize him at first—he looked so ordinary without that golden halo of light shining down on him. But it was him all right, sitting all cozied up to that redheaded woman who said she fell down her cellar stairs and couldn't walk a step until she got healed and started running back and forth on the stage shouting glory hallelujah.

Grandma remarked that she had lost her appetite, but Hursey and I each had a slice of warm crabapple pie with a scoop of vanilla ice cream oozing down the sides. After we finished eating, Grandpa poured a second cup of coffee into the beat-up thermos he'd used in the mines, and we got back on the road.

Feeling the hum of the tires on the blacktop, Hursey soon fell asleep, his legs sprawled halfway over my side of the seat. I thought about poking him to make him move over, but I never did. It wasn't like me to be that considerate. But I expected my brother was all worn out from one more disappointment in his life, although he never told me so and I never asked. Grandma began singing about how we'd understand it all by and by, her voice floating thin and warbly in the dark.

"Amen and amen," my grandpa said.

"Clev," Grandma said, "I'd just as soon you didn't start that."

Grandma picked up her darning needle and one of Grandpa's socks just like usual. Today she tuned the radio to Deke Godby's Gospel Hour. And just like usual, we never talked about our visit to Merle Hobart.

Ladies Don't Sweat

Taking advantage of the last hot days of summer, Grandpa held a revival where he'd preach every night for two weeks straight, begging and pleading with sinners to come forward and get saved so they wouldn't burn in an everlasting Hell. The meeting got pretty heated up, what with all the shouting and praying and preaching, and there was no breeze to damper down all those flame-filled words.

I started looking around for my favorite fan.

The only one left in the pew rack in front of me advertised Sunset Memorial Park Cemetery. Although the cemetery part appealed to me, somebody had scribbled all over the back. Grandma offered to trade me her Trublood Insurance Company fan, but I wasn't interested. I thought it said Troubled Insurance Company. Besides, I had my heart set on a fan two pews in front of us, the one with a blue-eyed Jesus in a royal blue robe, kneeling and looking up to a sky-blue Heaven.

Grandma said she wasn't putting up with my nonsense because all those fans worked the same and there wasn't one iota of difference and that I was just being picky for no good reason and she wasn't having me call unnecessary attention by traipsing all over the church because of some silly notion I had when there was a perfectly good fan right there. No sirree, she was not going to have it.

She knew I'd mind her, no question about it, but she also knew I'd pout all night. What would the church ladies think? She couldn't risk it.

"I guess you can this time, but you best get the one you want right off next time because there's just no sense in . . ."

She trailed off quick when Sister Wood came by with a question about the Home Missionary Society meeting at our house next week. Grandma was in charge of the missionary work and Grandpa was in charge of preaching, but in everything else he followed Grandma's lead like the faithful second-in-command he knew himself to be.

I smiled and said a big hello to Sister Wood to show Grandma I was over my pouting, then I hurried to get the Jesus fan.

The ladies fanned, swishing the cardboard back and forth in front of glistening faces. They dabbed runs of sweat from powdered necks with soft blue or peach or lilac handkerchiefs decorated with crocheted lace edges or embroidered flowers or maybe initials and birds.

"Ladies don't sweat," Grandma reminded me. "Horses sweat, men perspire, ladies glow."

Grandma had a natural dignity in how she carried herself, how she presented herself to the world. She said she didn't want the Lord catching her doing anything that didn't glorify His name. She didn't want anybody else to catch her either. She must have thought all the neighbors had a spy glass trained right on Grandpa as he went to feed the chickens and on her as she took the clothes off the line and even on me as I trudged up our red dog road to Sylvia Elementary School.

I wasn't supposed to kick too high or turn cartwheels or cross my legs when I sat down, and my scratchy wool skirt should always cover my knobby knees. I couldn't say heck or dang or anything else she thought substituted for a bad word.

Grandma didn't like for me to whistle either.

"A whistling girl or a crowing hen is neither fit for God nor men," she'd say.

Grandma put a lot of stock in what other people thought of us. She said a preacher's family should always be above reproach. And that was especially true for me and Vonnie.

Hursey, home for the summer, was threatening to tear a page out of the Bobbsey Twins book I was reading because he claimed I'd lost a piece of his jigsaw puzzle, while I tried to convince him that I hadn't done any such thing. The argument had progressed to the did, did not, did too stage. Grandma tired of our bickering and sent us outside so she could have some peace and quiet.

Right away Hursey let me know he wasn't going to play any silly girl games, so that left my favorite doll Peggy out, but he let me tag along. He took a suit of Grandpa's underwear off the clothesline and stuffed it with straw. The head was a flour sack with eyes and a mustache drawn on with a piece of coal. Hursey said the War would be over soon because Hitler had been killed.

When I asked who Hitler was, he said if I wasn't a dumb girl I'd know about Hitler. But I didn't care about Hitler anymore. I didn't care about being called a dumb girl.

The War would be over.

My mother would be coming home.

Hursey named the straw man Hitler and hung him from a noose looped over an apple tree branch. We marched around the tree, spitting out hateful words and throwing rotten apples at Hitler until we worked our little mob all the way up to an assassination. Hursey struck a stolen kitchen match and held the fire to Hitler's feet. The straw man flamed, slowly at first, then the whole body crackled and blazed. The wind picked up a burning clump of straw and dropped it on a pup tent we had set up to play army. It went up with an impressive whoosh.

Grandpa, hearing me squall, came running from the garden and grabbed the water hose to douse the flames before the roof of the fruit house caught fire. That's where we stored jars of canned goods and cured hams and barrels of apples and potatoes and cabbages, enough to see us through the winter.

Grandma told me if she ever caught me near a match I'd soon wish she hadn't.

I'd never had a spanking.

But that put the possibility in my mind.

Hursey was the one that made the straw Hitler. He had stolen the match and set the fire, but I never heard Grandma say a thing to him, although to be fair I suppose she could have. He got away with murder because he was deaf, or so I told myself. But deep down I believed it was because Grandma favored boys. She favored Uncle Vertis too. Everybody knew that, but Grandma claimed there was no truth to it whatsoever—she said she simply had higher expectations for the girls.

And we accepted it—higher expectations and all.

The War *was* soon over and Mother came home, blending back into our lives without fanfare. Of course, Grandma had cleaned the house top to bottom because she said she didn't want Mother to think we'd been living in a pigsty. And she fixed Mother's favorites for dinner—pot roast with potatoes and carrots and onions, tomato dumplings, mustard greens with fatback, macaroni and cheese, and cornbread muffins, finished off with lemon custard pie for dessert.

Although I had missed my mother, it took time to feel like she wasn't a visitor who'd be gone any day now. I was barely four when she left to go work as a Rosie the Riveter, so my memory of her living with us before she went to New York was dim. It was strange to hear her voice when I woke up in the mornings. My ears would perk up until I was sure I wasn't dreaming.

But I wasn't. She was home to stay.

And stay at home with us is what she did. After my father's death, Mother had an income from the almost brand-new Social Security program President Roosevelt had started, and she also provided the house we all lived in, which she had paid for with the thousand dollars she got from my father's death and the rest from money saved up from her Rosie the Riveter job. She worked part-time sales jobs off and on—Marie's Dress Shop, The Vogue, and a shoe store I don't remember the name of—but she was always home when I got out of school.

Everybody pitched in. Grandpa had a small pension from the mines, and Grandma sold butter and eggs to neighbors. Although it wasn't a lot of money, we didn't need a lot. We made or grew most everything we needed. And when she lived with us off and on, Aunt Lila contributed part of her income from working as a beauty operator. She was good at it, and the mayor's wife and other Beckley socialites lined up for her to do their hair. She bought me and Vonnie fancy fur-trimmed coats and muffs and boot skates.

But Aunt Lila didn't come home with Mother. Once again she'd stayed behind with Eddie Kamphey, the fellow she'd married up there in Buffalo, and we still weren't supposed to know about him or the marriage. So we pretended to be in the dark, our faces once again masks of not knowing. I don't know how my sister felt, but I liked knowing things I wasn't supposed to know. It made me feel like I had some power nobody else knew about.

Gypsy Skirt

Their wagons were painted with pictures of dancing girls, skirts billowed out, and of horses, walleyed and prancing, sleek dark men astride their bare backs. The caravan was at the bottom of the hill when I first spotted it. The horses, stocky and short-legged, strained as they muscled the heavy wagons up the sloping road. I ran straight home to tell Sissy the news before somebody beat me to it.

The gypsies were back.

Every year they came, usually toward spring, and watching their caravan ride into town was almost as good as the circus.

Like migrating birds returned to a favored nesting site, they camped in the same place each year, out in a field near Joe's Grocery. I couldn't go there or to Joe's either because I wasn't allowed to cross the 19-21 Bypass, which we called the hard road, and neither was Sissy, so we watched the gypsies from our side. They set up camp with practiced speed, and by nightfall there was a cluster of tents circled around the wagons and horses, a fire blazing in the center.

After a week or so, Carlotta appeared in my class at school. I didn't know how old she was, although she seemed older than the rest of us. She was a big girl, dark olive skin, hooded eyes that burned like coal, and heavy black hair that hung past her shoulders. When I stood next to her I felt colorless, my pale skin and eyes and hair boring. But what made Carlotta irresistible to me was the way she dressed. Gold hoops threaded through holes in her ears and colored bangles ringed both arms almost to her elbows.

One skirt I admired to the point of it being a sin had tiers of red and purple and magenta, each gathered onto the next, with sequins and ribbons and rickrack sewn in meandering rows. When she walked, gussets of lace flowed around her ankles and tiny mirrors on the hem danced in the light.

I wanted Grandma to make me a skirt like that, but she never would. She laughed and said she expected I'd be a sight to see swarping around in a gypsy skirt.

Carlotta didn't come to school every day, and she was way behind in most everything. Shy and quiet in class, she never answered a question or asked one either. I got to be her friend, at least sort of, because on the way home from school I told the boys who taunted her to shut up their big fat mouths. She slowed, deliberately I thought, so I could catch up, and we walked all the way to my house together. Carlotta waited while I ran in to ask Mother if I could go to Peggy's house. I would go to Peggy's after I went to Carlotta's, so I convinced myself it wasn't lying. It wasn't telling the whole truth either, but it was the best I could do.

Mother was sitting on the floor stripping layers of white enamel from the baseboards in the dining room. Our house had layers of enamel covering the oak floors and trim. Mother spent hours scraping that old paint off. She'd already finished the stairs and banister railings. It was a lot of work, but it would be worth it once done, or so she said.

She looked up, swiping her hair back with her sleeve. "You can go, but make sure you get yourself home on time."

I had the run of the neighborhood as long as I got home in time for meals, did not go inside anyone's house, and stayed within hollering distance. Otherwise, I needed permission. Mother and Grandma and Grandpa had to know where I was going and who I was going with and what I was going for and who else was going to be there. I tried to back out of the room before she had a chance to add her usual, "You be careful and don't you go anywhere else and you make sure you are back in this house before suppertime and don't you be running on that red dog road." She hollered after me, "I mean it now."

"Yes ma'am," I said, crossing my fingers ahead of time for lies I would tell.

I was pretty sure I was the only liar in our family. Grandpa was a Pentecostal preacher and he never lied, or at least I'd never caught him at it. He caught me though, and it wasn't the first time either. Before he handed me a nickel for the offering at church and one to spend at Beaver's General Store, he asked if I'd studied my Sunday school lesson.

"Yes sir," I said.

Grandpa allowed he didn't believe that was possible without divine intervention. He knew for a fact my lesson paper had been in the backseat of the car since services last Sunday and here it was Saturday already.

"I was planning on reading it. Honest I was. It was just a little white lie."

"I don't care how you color it," he said, "a lie is a lie."

He unpeeled the blue and white wrapper from a cake of Ivory soap. Although he had threatened to wash my mouth out before, this time he meant business. Hoping to wash the lying out of me once and for all, he ran the soap under the spigot to juice it up, then swiped it over my stuck-out tongue. I ran to the sink and splashed water in my mouth, sputtering and spitting bubbles. Seeing me froth at the mouth started Grandpa chuckling and that got me and Grandma to laughing. When we got over it, I complained my mouth tasted like old dishwater.

"Lies," my grandpa said, "should always leave a bad taste in your mouth."

In church the next day Grandpa preached on "The Truth about Lies." It could have been a coincidence.

On the way home we stopped for our usual cone of ice cream, and he didn't mention lying a single time. One thing about Grandpa, he didn't carry a grudge.

With the taste of soap hardly out of my lying mouth, I followed Carlotta through the field, then over the hard road, brazenly crossing the line I wasn't allowed to cross. A small tent near the highway had a sign out that said:

FORTUNES TOLD INSIDE
MADAM VADOMA KNOWS ALL,
SEES ALL, TELLS ALL

A woman in gypsy dress sat outside the tent husking a bushel basket of corn while she waited to unveil the past, present, and future for anyone with a couple of dimes to spare.

Carlotta weaved through a maze of tents and wagons and horses, and as I scrambled to keep up with her, I tried not to notice the dark eyes peering at me. We ducked inside a tent that had the front flap partway open. A rug unrolled on the dirt floor was spattered with red and purple cushions. An old woman dressed in a loose print dress like my grandma sometimes wore around the house sat carving some small thing she turned this way and that in her hand. Rings covered her fingers—one ivory with a skull carved in it, another a circle of dark wood, and others of turquoise and silver. Carlotta told me the woman was her grandmother, and she was carving faces on citronella nuts to sell or trade for food. Carlotta spoke in words I didn't understand, and the woman looked up and nodded, reaching out to touch my blonde hair.

The gypsies stirred up a fire in the center of the camp from embers left from the night before. A man appeared, holding chickens he killed and cleaned and cut into pieces with two knives he used at the same time. Grandma was good at cutting up chickens, but she could learn a thing or two from him. Others brought onions and carrots, and one man carried a burlap bag of potatoes thrown over his shoulder. A boy had a bunch of turnips that looked like they'd just been pulled out of the ground. One by one he tossed them in the air and the chicken man sliced off the root with a chop of his knife, catching the turnip before it could hit the dirt.

Everything went into the pot, including Madam Vadoma's corn, still on the cob, along with a generous amount of paprika and a handful of salt from a round box with a picture of a girl holding an umbrella, just like ours at home. A woman added something that looked like little onions, but Carlotta said it was garlic.

A boy, still wearing yesterday's dirt on his face, ran by.

"Lotty, there's a game over in the field," he hollered. He ran off, all elbows and knees, while Carlotta and I followed the noise to a bunch of girls and boys playing kickball behind the camp. They played rougher than I was used to, cussing and elbowing to get at the ball.

I didn't let on I thought that was rude.

Everybody's got their own ways of doing.

As the aroma of the stew spread, the gypsies began to gather around the fire, bowls and spoons clattering in their hands. Loaves of store-bought bread were stacked on a table next to the kettle. I watched as they put bread in their bowls, ladled stew on top, then added an ear of corn. A woman spooned a little into a bowl and handed it to me, watching as she motioned me to eat. It was different from anything I ever tasted—the ordinary vegetables and meat had lost all familiarity. A fire started at the back of my throat and burned down a wick to the bottom of my belly. My eyes watered, but I took another swallow.

The woman laughed, tilting her head back to show off a mouthful of gold teeth.

It was past time for me to start for home. I knew if I went to Peggy's now I'd be late getting home. Instead, I walked up her

street and touched the gate as I walked by so I could say I'd been by
her house if anybody asked, although I hoped they didn't. On the
way home I started to think I'd make a fine gypsy. I liked Carlotta's
skirts, and I liked the music and the dancing too. They had horses,
and I even had a taste for the heat of goulash stew. I'd already
decided to be a Methodist when I grew up, so I'd need to find out if
they allowed gypsies, although I didn't think it would be a problem.
I pulled the last piece of Double-Bubble from my pocket and put it
in my mouth to mask my gypsy breath.

Sometimes at night you could hear the music all the way to Sissy's
house, and we sat in her yard and listened until her daddy called us
in. When Grandpa drove home from prayer meeting, I'd ask him
to drive past the camp, although it was out of our way, so I could
see the gypsies around the fire, drawn to the light like a flock of
bright moths. One man played a little accordion Grandma said was
a concertina. Others fingered guitars strung with many strings. The
girls danced, lifting their chins and holding their arms up as they
circled the flames.

When the gypsies were in town, things went missing. Pants
and shirts disappeared off the Harveys' clothesline. The Bledsoes'
strawberry patch was picked clean one night, and Sissy's grandma,
Ma Moles, had her garden plundered and her pawpaw tree stripped
almost bare. But even worse, Grandpa said unless he was mistaken,
we were missing two white leghorns and a guinea hen. My heart
flopped over. In my mind I could see white feathers flying as the
man plucked the chickens for the stew. Caught in the web of my
deceit, I couldn't say a word.

One night someone dug up two potato hills in our garden,
and left several bunches of parsnips on the ground to ruin. Apples
thrown at Queenie lay rotting near the doghouse where she was
tied. Grandpa decided to see if he could catch the culprit.

Nothing happened the first night or the second, but the third night I woke up to Queenie barking. I sneaked down to the porch and saw Grandpa softly snoring in the swing, a flashlight in his hand and his double barrel shotgun propped between his knees. He woke right up when I touched his shoulder. When he heard Queenie, he told me not to move or he'd skin me alive when he got back. I made sure to stay put until he disappeared from sight around the far side of the house.

Crouched behind the blue hydrangea bush at the corner of the porch, I was near the garden but could still scoot back to the swing if Grandpa headed in my direction. I saw his flashlight search over the cabbage and potatoes and rhubarb.

Then it froze.

Grandpa hollered, and two shapes took off toward the tall rows of corn.

A shot blasted a hole through the quiet and the shadowy forms toppled.

My knees folded and I sat down so hard it knocked the wind out of me. I was too scared to breathe until I saw one of the thieves get on his knees and start sobbing and begging Grandpa not to shoot him, while the other one cowered nearby.

"Why, you're hardly more than babies," I heard Grandpa say. He knelt next to them, telling them they didn't have anything to be fearful of—he didn't plan on shooting either one of them or calling the law on them—at least not this time.

"I'm likely to do both if you boys come back here stealing out of my garden again. How old are you children anyway?"

The big boy said he was ten but his brother was only seven and wasn't allowed to be out at night. Grandpa took both boys by the hand and walked through the garden, the little one dragging a burlap bag behind.

"You tell me what you want, and I'll show you how to harvest so it won't damage the crop," Grandpa said.

Soon the boys filled the bag with potatoes and onions and carrots and ears of corn. Grandpa showed them how to tie their sack in the middle of a long pole so they could share the heavy load on the way home.

"A load is always lighter if it's shared. I want you to remember that. You want more, you knock and I'll give you what can be spared. I want to show you something else before you leave," he said, leading the boys over to where Queenie was tied.

He unhooked the leash, and Queenie, grateful for freedom, ran to the boys and started jumping up. Grandpa gave a hand signal and the dog sat down, watching Grandpa and waiting.

"This dog is part of our family, and I won't stand for her being tormented. She wants to be your friend. Go on over there now and get acquainted with her."

The smallest boy approached Queenie and put out a hand. Queenie closed her teeth gently over the dirty little arm, leading him around the yard and back to Grandpa.

"Her name is Queenie, and we're right fond of her. She'll do your bidding if you just ask her. Tell her to sit and she'll sit right down."

Recognizing the command, Queenie sat. The boys looked up at Grandpa wide-eyed.

"Okay, hold out your hand and she'll shake hands with you."

The older boy held out a hand and Queenie extended a paw.

"Now, boys, I don't want to hear tell of you mistreating this dog or any other living thing for that matter."

Grandpa put Queenie back on her leash and led the boys out to the road.

"You go straight home and don't be dallying along the way. And you remember that we have us a gentleman's agreement: You are welcome on my property anytime as long as you knock on my door first. Get along with you now."

I was wide awake after all the excitement, so I sat with Grandma and drank milk coffee while Grandpa told and retold the story of how he'd shot into the air to scare the boys.

"I hated like the dickens to have to scare 'em like I did, but them little hooligans needed somebody to get their attention. I'm hoping they'll think twice next time, but there's no telling. What they need is somebody at home to jerk a knot in their tail and straighten them out, but I expect that's where they're learning their thievery."

"If you caught me stealing, you'd more than likely wring my neck," I said.

"More than likely," Grandpa agreed, "but that's because you been taught right from wrong. Maybe them little fellows don't know better."

Grandma said she didn't want to hear any more foolishness from me and Grandpa about wringing people's necks. She had her no-nonsense face on, so Grandpa aimed a yes ma'am in her direction.

"Tell it again," I begged.

"I figure you know it well as I do, you do the telling this time. I've plumb wore my teller out."

Every week or so after, always just before dawn, we heard a tapping at the front door, getting a little louder if Grandpa didn't hurry down. He pulled pants and suspenders over his long johns and went out to help his new friends fill their bag. Grandma followed him downstairs and put a pot of coffee on the stove. Sometimes she gave the boys a sack of oatmeal cookies or a pint of damson preserves, and a time or two she gave them a basket of eggs.

We never had another chicken disappear.

Carlotta didn't play with me at school, at least not much, but one day at recess she joined me at the seesaw. When the girl on the other end hopped off, Carlotta caught the board and held it until my feet were on solid ground. I liked that about her—she wasn't the kind of person who'd get off the seesaw and leave the person on the other end to hit the dirt. She held out her closed hand and passed something to me, folding my hand around it before she walked away. I opened my fist and saw a citronella nut like the one her grandmother carved that day. She didn't come back to school after that. And one night soon after, the camp disappeared.

I never saw Carlotta again.

But I still imagined myself dancing with her, chin up and eyes flashing, mirrored skirts swirling in the light of a gypsy fire.

Birds of a Feather

Aunt Lila was a beauty operator, Licensed and Board Certified. My mother's older sister by five years, she came to live with us because she was between husbands again. Eddie Kamphey hadn't suited her, at least not for long, so she'd left him in New York where she'd found him.

Absentmindedly rubbing at the red mark her hairnet had left on her forehead, Aunt Lila stood gazing out the kitchen window. She needed to come up with a showstopper for the big hair styling contest being held in Charleston, the state capital, the following week. We watched as Buttermilk, my scruffy orange tomcat, dodged a pair of blue jays that dived at him, protecting the nest they'd built in the cherry tree. All of a sudden she clapped her hands together, stirring up a whiff of the Lucky Strikes she tried to hide with dabs of Evening in Paris secreted in her purse along with a slim black cigarette holder.

With a perfectly manicured hand she reached for a cup and saucer and poured the last of the coffee that was keeping hot on the stove, waiting for the grounds to settle before taking her first disappointing sip.

"This stuff could choke a horse." She made a sourpuss face as she glanced at me.

Hunched over the kitchen table, she started to sketch, but I couldn't see. I begged, but she wouldn't even let me peek.

Aunt Lila didn't drive, so Mother was taking her to pick up my brother's girlfriend, Rayjeana, who would be Aunt Lila's model for the contest.

Rayjeana got in the backseat with me, hair the color of honey hanging halfway down her back. I noticed her eyes were robin's egg blue. While I watched, she squeezed a little Vaseline on her finger and flicked her lashes with it. She told me not to tell about the Vaseline, and I wouldn't. Well, nobody but Sissy. After all, she was my best friend and we told each other everything.

Or maybe I'd simply slick the Vaseline on my eyelashes and wait for Sissy to notice. Lately I'd been thinking I wanted to grow up to look like Rayjeana instead of Lana Turner, but the spattering of rusty freckles across my nose gave me cause to worry.

I snuck an admiring glance at Rayjeana's unspattered summer nose.

Aunt Lila led Rayjeana into the sitting room off our downstairs bedroom. She'd set up shop there, littering the room with shoeboxes overflowing with brushes and metal clamps and bobby pins. After a couple of hours, she hollered for us to come see. Mother walked in first and gasped. Grandma said, "Oh my word." Vonnie, just ahead of me, stopped so sudden I bumped into her. I stood on my tiptoes so I could see over her shoulder.

Rayjeana sat with her back to us, facing a big oval mirror borrowed from the mahogany dresser in the spare bedroom. When I saw her reflected back at me, I had no doubt.

Aunt Lila's hairdo was bound to call attention.

We got up early on the day of the contest and started driving the sixty or so miles to Charleston, little more than a two-hour trip if the weather and our luck held out. The weather was fine, but before we got halfway, one of the back tires started making a thumpity-thump sound. Mother eased into a Gulf station that advertised "MECHANIC ON DUTY—DAY & NITE."

"I knew I should have checked about that tire," Mother said to herself.

"Then why on earth didn't you?" Aunt Lila asked. "You know I can't be late."

"Maybe I have better things to do than keep this car running to cart you around."

"Hogwash," Aunt Lila said. "If you did, you'd be doing them."

A man ambled out, adjusting a dirty sling on his arm as he eyed our sorry-looking tire. "Mechanic ain't showed up. Off hunting's my guess."

Mother looked over at the sign, then back at the man.

"Yes ma'am, I know what it says. But it don't mean diddly to that boy during squirrel season."

Without another word Mother pulled the jack from the trunk and positioned it so the weight wouldn't bend the frame. She jacked the car up until the wheels cleared the ground, loosened the lug nuts with a wrench as long as her forearm, and wrestled the faulty tire off, replacing it with the spare, which didn't look all that much better but would have to do. She placed the jack back in the trunk and threw the old blanket she'd used to protect her nice skirt and blouse over it. It wasn't new, but it was one of her favorite outfits, a jade-green skirt with a soft ivory blouse printed with ivy leaves. Green was the color she looked best in—everybody said so.

"Y'all go on to the restroom so we don't have to stop again," she told us, "but don't be dawdling around in there."

Vonnie went in while I waited outside. There was a big old horsefly buzzing around when it was my turn. After shooing him out, I put the seat down and spread layers of toilet paper on it to keep from sitting on the wood, although I still just crouched over it. The seat sprung right up again and smacked my bottom, layers of toilet paper drifting onto the floor. I yanked my underpants up and pulled my dress down, my slip still bunched around my waist. The soap container was empty, but I didn't care—filling station soap always smelled like tar anyway. I ran my hands under the spigot, not even singing "Twinkle, Twinkle, Little Star" to make sure I'd washed long enough. I cranked the cloth-towel roll on the wall looking for a reasonably clean place to use. Giving up, I dried my hands on my dress.

"You notice anything in there?" Vonnie asked.

"You mean that big old fly?" I was a little peeved she hadn't warned me about the toilet seat, not that I would have warned her, but still, a big sister had an obligation. Grandma said so.

"No, dummy, that toilet seat!"

"Oh, I've seen those before over at the Black Knight Country Club," I lied.

I'd forgotten to cross my fingers, so I had to count that as a real lie.

Vonnie looked suspicious, but since it was half true, she couldn't be sure I was lying. Ann Nuckols, a classmate whose father was a state senator, had invited a bunch of us to attend her birthday party at the Black Knight Country Club. I had been there, but Vonnie hadn't, so she didn't know they had ordinary toilet seats like everybody else.

Once we got on the road again, Aunt Lila doled out buttered cornbread with peach preserves and whole deviled eggs made from halves she had stuck back together and wrapped in waxed paper for the trip. There were jars of sweet tea with lemon and a bag of gingersnaps. She passed us a wet washcloth when we finished. Rayjeana got carsick so we had to stop two more times for her to throw up. Mother said more than likely it was just a bad case of nerves.

The contest was held in a school auditorium on the edge of Charleston. The master of ceremonies, a tall, skinny man whose pants were so short I could see flashes of his bright yellow socks, introduced the first model. Her hair was finger-waved back into a cascade of silver blue curls. The style was "Niagara Falls," but he pronounced it "Niagara Fallth." Vonnie looked at me and rolled her eyes. Then came a blonde woman with her hair braided into a lattice design. That hairdo was named "Heidi," which he could say just fine. The next model had black hair lacquered into a smooth fat bun, with chopsticks crossed in it. She wore a red satin housecoat wrapped with a stiff wide sash to look like a kimono. This one was called "Geisha Girl." He said "Geitha Girl." There were a bunch more hairdos, but "Geisha Girl" was the only one I was worried about. I noticed her wood shoes were the kind I'd seen on pictures of Dutch girls. I didn't know if that would count against her, but I hoped so.

Finally Rayjeana, wearing the long lavender-blue dress she'd made for prom the year before, floated onto the stage. Her hair was back-combed into a bird's nest swirled high on top of her head. She curtsied, dipping low to show off three egg-shaped curls inside the nest. A blue-feathered bird, one I'd last seen on our Christmas tree, perched on the side.

"Thith lath one here ith 'Bluebeard of Happineth,'" the man said.

Vonnie kept digging her elbow in my side, but I didn't dare look at her for fear I'd bust out laughing.

There was a smattering of applause.

Huddled together, the judges looked at index cards they'd made notes on and shook their heads up and down or sideways, depending on which hairdo it was they were talking about. Finally the man with the yellow socks asked the beauty operators and their models to line up on stage for the winners to be announced. I don't remember who got honorary mention or third place, but Geisha was the second place winner. I held my breath.

"And the firth plath winner . . . Bluebeard of Happineth!"

Mother and Vonnie and I let out a big whoop and embarrassed ourselves when people turned around to look at us. Aunt Lila and Rayjeana, still on stage, were more ladylike.

On the way home we imitated the yellow-sock man saying the words all funny and getting the name of the hairdo wrong. Mother told us to quit it right now, that we ought to be ashamed of ourselves for mocking somebody's affliction, but she had laughed too, although she claimed it wasn't about that at all.

I thought Aunt Lila's trophy was a beauty, but she said that wobbly thing was so tacky she had half a mind to let them put "Bluebeard of Happineth" on it. I said oh, no she couldn't, but oh, yes she could if she wanted, she declared, now mocking me. We laughed at that and at Mother's imitation of the look on the slack-jawed man's face when she changed the tire. And when Vonnie told about getting whacked by the commode seat, we laughed some more.

Mother said we were all right giddy from the excitement.

Rayjeana said if she laughed anymore she was going to pee her pants. "That's just your nerves again," Mother said, but she pulled into a diner called Karol's Kupboard just in case. Since we were already stopped, Aunt Lila offered to treat for supper. I ordered a fried baloney sandwich on white bread with potato chips and a cherry coke, foods Grandma wouldn't allow. Mother gave us each a nickel to play the jukebox attached to the wall of our booth. She wouldn't let me play the Andrews Sisters singing "Drinking Rum and Coca-Cola," although I didn't know why not; it was on the radio all the time. So I played something else, but I don't remember what.

I yawned wide.

Mother said for me to close my mouth before a moth flew in.

Words blurred into faraway sounds that made no sense. Something about remembering to check the oil and yellow socks and the sandman. My eyelids closed over gritty eyes, and I soon fell asleep with my head on Vonnie's shoulder.

I dreamed I was just like my Aunt Lila, except I was driving the car as I waved to Lana Turner and Rayjeana, a long black cigarette holder between the fingers of my perfectly manicured hand.

The Living and the Deaf

Grandpa was just back from a trip to the Beaver sisters' general store. He watched Grandma pull sugar and flour and coffee and Crisco out of the paper poke and set it on the table. The last thing out was a can of Clabber Girl baking powder.

"Clev, surely you know I don't use anything but Rumford." There was an accusing edge to her voice.

"Couldn't be helped. They were all out."

"Well, don't ever buy that Clabber Girl again. That stuff's not fit to eat."

With all the baking that went on at our house, it wasn't long before me and Grandpa were sent to the store for more baking powder. When we got back, Grandma unpacked the Ipana toothpaste, Jergen's lotion, cornmeal, Goody's headache powder, and a jar of Postum, a powdered hot drink made of roasted grain. Grandpa had grown fond of it when coffee was rationed during the War and still drank it from time to time. "Easier on the gut," he said, rubbing his hand over his aching belly.

"They won't get any Rumford until the end of the week," Grandpa explained before Grandma had a chance to ask.

"What did you get me then?"

"Didn't get none of it. You told me not to."

"For goodness' sake, Clev, you know I can't make biscuits

without baking powder. I don't see why on earth you didn't bring me what they had. I could've made do."

Grandpa winked at me.

"Guess me and you better go get your Grandma some of that sorry old Clabber Girl if we want any biscuits around this house." He chuckled as he went out the door, me right behind him.

Somehow Grandma managed to make biscuits despite having to use the Clabber Girl.

"Not fit to eat," she muttered, dumping the pan of biscuits in a big bowl. She folded a napkin over them, either to keep them warm or hide them. I wasn't sure which. When the biscuits were passed around, I could not see one bit of difference.

But I kept that to myself.

Hursey had been home from boarding school all summer, filling the house with his friends. How word got around I didn't know, but it never failed. Half a dozen teenage boys, most a few years older than him, soon had their feet stuck under Grandma's supper table, their hands soaring and diving like birds. You'd think a table full of deaf boys would be quiet, but not so. Our house soon filled with their boisterous laughter and grunts, their fists slapping into palms for emphasis, faces contorted into exaggerated expressions of anger and joy and surprise. Those who could speak often talked out loud while signing, sometimes all at once, and those who couldn't speak mimed the words. My brother had started at West Virginia School for the Deaf and Blind in Romney, West Virginia, when he was seven, coming home only for Christmas and summer vacations. Grandma said it was a crying shame families had to send little children away to boarding school where they didn't know a solitary soul. But Mother really didn't have a choice. It was the only place Hursey could get an education. He had started school late like most deaf kids we knew, but even still, he excelled there, skipping several grades.

At Romney, in addition to the usual reading, writing, and arithmetic, students were taught a trade. The boys who were average or below were trained to be bakers. Another choice, reserved for the smart ones, was to work in the print shop. There may have been other choices, but those are the ones I remember.

My brother was trained as a printer.

I could spell the alphabet on my hands before I knew how to say my ABCs, and I learned a lot of signs, but I never got real good at it. Because my brother had already learned how to talk before he was deaf, his speech was pretty good and he read lips, so we could talk with him without signing.

Besides, I was seven years younger, and he ignored me as much as I'd let him.

Although I was always glad to see him, I sometimes liked it better when he wasn't there. My brother sucked up all the attention when he was home. And Grandma liked him best, although she'd never admit to it.

"Why, look at the shape he's in," she'd say.

I was never sure what she meant by that. Hursey looked in fine shape to me. The hearing girls in East Beckley were always trying to get him to notice them. They'd come around pretending to have an interest in me and Vonnie, teaching us to twirl a baton, or play badminton with us in the yard, all the while casting glances to see if Hursey was watching. He was.

Hursey liked to play the field. I never knew him to go steady with anyone while he was in school, but he may have at Romney and I didn't know about it. He only dated Rayjeana for a month or so before he lost interest and started seeing Dorothy Wiseman, who sometimes taught Sunday school at St. Mary's. Grandma liked to see him going out with good Christian girls like Rayjeana and Dorothy, even if both of them were Methodists, but Dorothy was her favorite—maybe because she lived right next door and Grandma could keep an eye on them. She also liked two other East Beckley girls he dated, Sue Cox and Eldana Jones. But like most teenage summer romances, they all ended when summer did and Hursey had to go back to school.

Mother was driving Hursey back to Romney, and Grandma and me and Vonnie had come along to keep her company. Besides, we weren't ones to turn down a trip out of town. He'd just got his driver's license, so Mother let him drive before we hit any bad roads. We couldn't find an Esso station, but we spotted a Sunoco where the sign said gas was thirteen cents a gallon. Grandma said she expected we could get it cheaper on down the road a piece. She always said that, but we pulled in anyway. Mother leaned over to tell the man to fill it up and please check the oil.

"What's wrong with him? He deaf and dumb?" The man was asking Mother, but he nodded toward my brother.

My brother could read lips, so he knew what the man said. He also knew that dumb meant a person couldn't speak, but it was still a word he was sensitive to. Besides, he wasn't dumb. He knew how to talk before the meningitis left him deaf, so he could speak quite well.

Hursey was used to being insulted and slighted. Usually the offender didn't intend any insult, although some did, but Hursey didn't make any allowance for ignorance—he took offense either way.

I saw the red rising up his neck.

He threw the car door open and got out. "Excuse me," he said, brushing past the man. He walked over to the pop machine and lifted the lid, putting coins in the slot before jerking out a bottle and using the opener attached to the machine to pry off the cap. When he started back, the man turned and hurried inside the station, leaving his helper to finish up. After my brother was back in the car, I asked him if he was fixing to punch that man in the nose.

"I don't know," he replied. "I hadn't quite decided."

The boy picked up a pop bottle of vinegar water and a crumpled page of yesterday's news to clean the windshield and then opened the front door and swept the carpet with a whisk broom that was worn down almost to the handle. When he looked back at me and Vonnie, I noticed he was double cross-eyed, both eyes pointing toward his nose. He wore glasses that magnified his eyes, making them the one thing on his face you had to look at, especially if you tried not to. I stared back because I didn't get to glance away before he caught me watching him. If I looked away, he'd think it was because of him being cross-eyed. I got out of it when Mother came back from paying for the gas and passed around a pack of Black Jack gum.

Vonnie told me later she thought the boy was kinda cute. I didn't mention about his eyes.

That was just between me and him.

After settling in at the tourist home, we ate lamb stew with the family that lived there. That was something we didn't eat at home. I was willing to give it a try, but Vonnie, always a picky eater, wouldn't eat a bite. Grandma said she guessed it wouldn't hurt if she skipped the meat this once, but Mother said she at least had to taste it. "Just one bite," she said, holding out a fork with a little piece of meat on it. Vonnie refused to open her mouth. Mother, not wanting Vonnie to show herself at the people's house, let her get away with it.

Vonnie started singing under her breath, "My sister ate a little lamb, little lamb, little lamb, My sister ate a little lamb . . ."

Grandma gave her a look and she stopped.

We took Hursey back to his dormitory before curfew, while we slept in four-poster beds so tall we had to use steps to climb in and out.

Romney had a football game the next afternoon. My brother was on the team and this was the first game he'd played. The weather had turned from fall crisp to winter cold overnight. Vonnie and I wore undershirts and scratchy wool sweaters layered under heavy coats, and two pairs of socks. We folded scarves into triangles and tied them under our chins. We looked like the round Russian dolls someone had given me, the little wooden ones that fit inside each other. I lost a glove climbing up the bleachers and had to keep my hand in my pocket to keep it from freezing. Vonnie told me to use one of my socks as a mitten, and that helped.

She gave me a quick once-over.

"You look queer as a clown. Put the other green sock on so you'll have matching hands instead of one red and one green. Thank goodness no one I know is here to see you right now because if a one of them did I would simply die."

According to my sister, I spent a good deal of time trying to embarrass her.

Hursey, smaller and younger than many of the other players, sat on the bench most of the time. Toward the end of the game he was sent in to kick the extra point after Romney tied the score. He lined up behind the ball and kicked it wobbling toward the goal where it hit the goalpost and fell short.

Romney lost the game.

Hursey, overly sensitive and impulsive, never played football again.

There was to be a dance in the Romney gymnasium. Since Mother had volunteered to chaperone, she said Vonnie and I could go, although Grandma was dead set against it. I promised myself I would pout for a whole month if Grandma talked her out of letting us go.

"Kathleen, you go on ahead and leave the children with me," Grandma said. "I'll see to it they have their baths and get to bed on time. They don't have any business being around a bunch of teenagers wiggling to music that's not fit to be heard anyway."

I held my breath.

Mother turned from helping me with a broken shoelace and looked straight at Grandma. "They can walk through the doors of this school or their own anytime they're open," she said, "and it doesn't matter what for, be it a ballgame, school play, or a dance where everybody there is wiggling. That's the end of it so far as I'm concerned." She went back to tying my broken shoelace together and putting it back in my shoe.

Grandma didn't say one word.

It wasn't in her nature to fight losing battles.

"Come back over here and let me fix your hair so you don't embarrass your brother," Mother said. "You look like you been wallering around on your head."

I was always getting accused of embarrassing somebody.

Hursey got all spiffed up in a new olive-drab suit. The cuffs of his white shirt shot past his jacket sleeves to show off gold-colored cufflinks with onyx stones. His tie was a paisley of gold and blue and black. Just like our father had done, he wore his belt buckle skewed off to the side and the face of his watch turned to the inside of his wrist. When Mother noticed, she smiled and shook her head.

The girls, dressed in pastel taffeta and netting, huddled on one side of the room so the boys couldn't read their hands as they signed. The boys did the same thing, acting like they could care less, but glancing over their shoulders to see if any of the girls were looking their way.

The Victrola was placed on the hardwood floor of the basketball court, the volume turned up full blast. You couldn't hear yourself, but not many cared. "Boogie Woogie Bugle Boy of Company B" blasted out, the sound pounding in my head and vibrating through the soles of my shoes up to my knees.

My feet started tapping all by themselves.

Hursey's best friend, Billy, black pompadour slicked high with Brylcreem pomade, took the long walk across the oak floor to a girl in a yellow gown. He led her onto the open floor where he started twirling her out and back and under his arm, all the while shifting his feet to match the beat.

"I didn't know Billy could jitterbug like that!" Mother said.

I'd never heard of the jitterbug before, but I couldn't take my eyes off the two of them. When the song ended, they walked off to stomping feet and waving hands. Other couples ventured out for the next dance, a slow number Billy danced with a pretty dark-haired girl. Hursey sat on the sidelines and moped the whole time, begging until Mother agreed to take him back to the dormitory. When Vonnie and I complained about having to leave early, Mother said it was time to go anyway. She wouldn't want Grandma getting herself all in a tizzy about us being out half the night.

Still sulking about missing the extra point the day before, Hursey hardly said a thing when we picked him up for breakfast. Hardly ate anything either, which was a shame because Mother always treated us to breakfast at a pancake place before we left.

After we said our goodbyes and promised to write, although I never did that I remember, nor did Hursey, we started for home.

It was a trip we made many times over the years.

One that started out full of promise, but always ended feeling empty.

Even though Hursey hadn't started to school at Romney until he was seven, he still managed to graduate when he was seventeen, skipping a couple of grades along the way.

After he graduated, Hursey got a scholarship to Gallaudet College in Washington, D.C., where again many of his classmates were several years older. As part of freshman hazing or maybe it was a fraternity, he had to stand on a busy street corner holding a sign with a picture of a naked woman on it. And he got arrested. Well, not really arrested, but picked up by the police. The local police gave the Gallaudet kids some leeway, so they simply escorted him back to campus and left him with the dean, who gave him a talking to. My brother's black-and-white sense of justice required that everyone involved be punished, but for some reason he was the only one who got in trouble, or so he claimed.

That's when he decided to leave.

Unable to realize how that foolhardy decision would affect his life, leave he did. Mother had sent him money to buy a typewriter for his birthday. Instead, he bought a one-way Greyhound ticket home.

No matter what Mother said, he refused to go back.

So my brother would not be a doctor, lawyer, merchant, or chief.

Instead, he got a job working as a printer. He was good at it. Good at layout, and lightning fast on the linotype machine. So good that when his supervisor left, he was asked to train the new one.

"If I can train a new boss, why can't I be one?"

It was a question he asked many times over the years.

But there was no good answer—at least none that satisfied him. Haunted by his deafness and his dreams, my brother lived between what he called the living and the deaf, never feeling at ease in either world.

Lonely Hearts
Club Man

The man standing at our front door clutched a forlorn bunch of posies in his fist. Through the screen I watched the small animal squatting on his head scooch forward, ready to leap onto my face and chew my nose off. I took a quick step back and stepped on Aunt Lila's toe, causing her to yelp—or it could be the varmint caused it. Then I realized it was only a ratty toupee, no longer matched to the graying tufts that stuck out over his ears.

I admit to feeling a little let down.

Aunt Lila smiled her toothiest smile. "I'm Kathleen, Lila's twin," she lied. "No doubt you'd be the gentleman from the Romeo Lonely Hearts Club." She kept right on lying, not allowing time for him to answer. "Lila felt terrible she couldn't be here to meet you in person, but she had to travel to Bluefield to get the children on real short notice. Of course you wouldn't know a thing about them, now would you? Our Aunt Pearlie went on to Glory sudden-like, rest her soul, and left her brood to Lila, her being barren and all. Eight boys, and quite a handful if I do say so. Be a nice ready-made family for some lucky man, don't you think?"

He squirmed and inched back toward the steps as she spoke.

"I'd ask you in for a cup of coffee, but of course you'll be wanting to get back to your busy life in Wichita. If you back-track up that red dog to Worley Road, you can catch the same bus back to town if you don't dawdle. It does a turnaround over by the Pinecrest TB Sanitarium and ought to be heading this way any minute now. I'll be sure to give Lila your regards. Don't you be a stranger now," she hollered after him.

He practically tripped over his feet scurrying down the porch steps. Aunt Lila closed the door, grinning at me like a possum.

I had a new level of admiration. That lie had come to her all in one piece.

It was a relief to know I got it honest.

The ad was in the back of a magazine: "Alone and lonely? Looking for a pen pal? Or maybe more? Sign up to Romeo's Lonely Hearts Club and correspond with the likeminded utilizing our safe and confidential service. Romeo Lonely Hearts Club guarantees your satisfaction one hundred percent or double your money back."

Here's how it worked. For a small fee, the folks at Romeo's Lonely Hearts Club would act as a go-between, relaying messages back and forth. Aunt Lila invested two dollars in her future and sent off the application, including a few words to stir up some interest: "Gay divorcee ready to find true love—this slim, blue-eyed beauty operator is seeking to meet a man of substance. No louts, boozers, gamblers, lotharios, unemployed, or left-handed."

I asked her what a lothario was and what was wrong with being left-handed.

"Nothing personal against the left-handed," she said. "It's not their fault. But bumping elbows with a leftie the rest of my life would sooner or later get on my nerves."

She didn't tell me what a lothario was, and I forgot to ask her again.

Before long the Romeo Lonely Hearts Club sent Aunt Lila a letter telling her about the men who were waiting to make her acquaintance. She could write to as many as she wanted, signing each letter with the number the Romeo people assigned to her. You could keep your real name a secret.

She'd done exactly what they said—and she'd told the truth about herself too.

Well, pretty much.

She hadn't said that she was a smoker or that she'd been married not just once, but twice before. I wasn't sure leaving out those details was the same as lying, but I hoped she'd crossed her fingers just in case.

After the toupee man, her responses came in batches:

Dear 109,

Let me introduce myself proper-like. I'm a man of medium height and build and means. My job for the better part of two years is to travel around the town filling vending machines with different brands of cigarettes. But I am quitting it since I recently broke the vile habit that I acquired in the U.S. Army, which I am no longer in since I lost my right eye in the War. No more coffin nails for me. Only nicotine-free need answer.

Number 554

She wadded that one up and did an overhand shot into the wastebasket.

Aunt Lila was a smoker, although she pretended not to be, while I pretended I didn't know a thing about the Lucky Strikes she kept in her purse at all times.

"Nothing worse than a recently reformed man," she said, looking to me for agreement.

There were two other letters in this batch:

Dear Miss,

I'm a God-fearing man who is seeking holy matrimony with a thrifty woman of quiet nature who is a excellent cook, keeps a orderly house and performs other wifely duties without a rebellious spirit as dictated by scripture. If you doubt this is the true word of God, search out Ephesians 5:22-24.

No. 368

That letter was wadded up too.

Aunt Lila said she hadn't been divorced twice for nothing.

"I haven't kowtowed to anyone so far, and I'm not about to start now. Don't you ever kowtow either," she told me.

I promised I wouldn't.

Along with *harlot*, which Grandpa had used in his last sermon, I added *kowtow* and *lothario* to words I needed to look up in the dictionary.

The next letter sounded a little better:

Dear #109,

You must be a beautiful woman with a name such as that. Ha Ha. My hope is that you will wish to further our acquaintance. I am in retail sales with Sears Roebuck & Co. where I am in haberdashery. So, hats off to you. Ha Ha.

#716

After a suitable period of time of letters going back and forth, Aunt Lila decided to meet #716. She liked a man with a sense of humor.

Having learned her lesson by letting the man we called Romeo One come to the house, she arranged to meet up with Romeo Two at the Tip-Top Café downtown. If things didn't go well, she could make a getaway.

She spent an extra-long time getting ready for her date, although every time I called it that she told me to quit it because it wasn't one. After she'd tried on most everything in her closet, Mother and Vonnie and I agreed she should wear a fitted navy-blue dress with a sweetheart neckline. Grandma liked another blue dress with a flared skirt. Blue was Aunt Lila's best color—it matched her eyes.

Ignoring all of us, she decided on a sky-blue dress, topping it with a yellow jacket with white piping and buttons that looked like daisies, saying it made her feel like the spring chicken Mother kept telling her she no longer was. Mother was five years younger.

"Well, you're right about one thing," Mother said. "It does make you look like a chicken."

Aunt Lila took the jacket off and put it back in the closet, and Mother nodded approval.

Grandma said they pecked back and forth worse than me and Vonnie.

As soon as we heard the door bang shut, we all headed to the front room. Aunt Lila was back from her date, or whatever it was she wanted us to call it. She flopped into a chair and threw her legs over the padded arm, kicking her black-and-white spectator heels to the floor and wiggling her stockinged toes.

"He seemed all right at first, real pleasant and easygoing. But then he started in telling jokes. And every one of them about hats. Another hat joke out of him and I'd have gone plumb batty."

"Tell me a hat joke!" I begged.

"Okay," she said, "but hold your nose—I wanted to wear my camouflage hat today, but I couldn't find it.

"After he told that joke he'd thrown his head back and guffawed. No," she said, "it sounded more like a mule braying."

I thought of Flapjack, my Uncle Vertis's old mule, stretching his neck and pulling his lips back to show his teeth.

"Oh, he was full of hat jokes, just full of them," Aunt Lila said.

"Tell some more," I pleaded.

"Just one more," she said, making her sourpuss face. "I'm sick and tired of hat jokes. What did the hat say to the tie?"

"I don't know," I said, eager to get to the funny part.

"You hang around, and I'll go on a head."

I threw my head back and laughed, trying to sound like Flapjack.

Aunt Lila rolled her eyes.

I guessed I'd have to practice.

"There were a bunch more jokes," she said, "each sillier than the last. After every one he made that gosh-awful braying sound. By the time he'd told half a dozen, his face started to take on the look of a mule. His teeth turned long and yellow, and an unruly hank of hair fell across his eyes like a forelock."

Aunt Lila told the man she felt a spell of her malaria coming on. Too bad she had to run out on him like this, but she needed to get home to take some of those horse pills that kept her from throwing up all over kingdom come. She hoped she could make it. Heaving convincingly, she'd grabbed her pocketbook and headed out of the Tip-Top at a trot, turning toward the bus stop on Main Street.

Disheartened after her visits from Romeos One and Two, she came close to giving up. And she did for a while, but not because of them.

Grandma had heard on the radio about a Lonely Hearts Club killer.

The next day the story was on front pages everywhere. A man and woman who met through a Lonely Hearts Club, but not the Romeo one, had been arrested for killing a whole bunch of people.

Grandma said the details of what those two did were too awful to speak of. Maybe so, but I'd overheard the neighbor women chattering about it like a bunch of magpies. "Little pitchers have big ears," they'd say, and stop talking when I came around. But I had heard enough to have a good idea what they were gossiping about. Grandma, who always gave folks the benefit of the doubt, said she expected it was just idle talk.

I had my own opinion about that.

Then another letter came.

When Aunt Lila noticed that his number was the same as our house number at 211 Bibb Avenue, she took it as a sign to give Romeo Lonely Hearts one more try. After all, the killers were both locked away in jail.

Dear Miss 109,

I am a retired New York City cop seeking friendship
leading to possible marriage with a good-looking
woman of wholesome background who is willing to
relocate if need be.

Respectfully, 211

So Aunt Lila began to write to 211, and he to answer back, each
letter deepening their interest. Before too long, 211 became Charles
Landwehr. And then Charles Landwehr was coming all the way
from Newark, New Jersey, for a visit. He was Romeo Three.

The house, of course, had to be deep cleaned. Grandma was in
charge, but she recruited me and Vonnie and Grandpa as reluctant
helpers. Since it was time for fall cleaning anyway, I was prepared for
the scrubbing and beating and dusting and polishing we always did.

But this time Grandma went a step further.

She decided to take down the beds so she could clean under and
around and behind them. I blamed my friend Peggy Blevins for this.
One day she mentioned taking down the beds to do deep cleaning,
and I made the mistake of telling Grandma, who soon decided she
needed to take our beds down too. Mattresses were stripped bare and
vacuumed then turned head to foot and top to bottom before being
placed back on the newly hosed off bedsprings. All the bed covers
were washed and hung to dry in the sun. Grandma wouldn't take a
backseat to anybody when it came to cleaning.

Uncle Vertis, Grandma's only son and my mother's big brother,
had come to borrow Mother's electric drill from her Rosie the
Riveter days but got dragged into helping take down beds. Mother
said it was the least he could do—always borrowing her stuff then
not returning it—and he better have that drill back to her come
Saturday or it would be the last he'd ever see of it. Uncle Vertis
pretended to look scared.

Charles Landwehr asked Aunt Lila to find a room for him at a
nearby tourist home. Mother took Aunt Lila and me to check out
the Morning Glory establishment over on the By-Pass to see if it

was suitable. Although the room was full of curlicues and knick-knacks, it was both clean and close by. It would do fine.

Finally, the day arrived.

Aunt Lila had given herself a permanent wave a few weeks before. To make sure the smell was gone, she poured water mixed with lemon juice over her head. She pushed finger waves into her damp hair, using metal clamps to pinch them in place, then pin-curled the rest, securing each curl with two crossed bobby pins. After she sat under the hairdryer, she finger combed through the tight ringlets until she had a soft halo of curls around her head.

When Grandma finished cleaning, the house reeked of floor wax and vinegar. She put a pan of water on to boil, adding a sprinkling of cloves and cinnamon and vanilla. Satisfied, she turned her attention to the kitchen and began fixing supper for Charles Landwehr's arrival. She hoped he wasn't Jewish because she'd baked a ham. Landwehr didn't sound Jewish, but you couldn't always be sure. To be on the safe side, she put a fat hen in the oven. There was dressing and gravy to go along with the ham and chicken, potato salad, pickled green beans, baked candied apples, and corn on the cob. Mother made strawberry shortcake and whipped up some cream. It was Aunt Lila's favorite.

Grandma lifted the lid on one side of the stove with a poker and filled the opening with kindling from the wood box. Our oven door hadn't closed right for some time, so she grabbed a piece of kindling to prop it up. Busy mixing up a pan of cornbread, she turned her back on the open door just long enough for Buttermilk to crawl inside the cavernous space, still warm from the earlier baking. Without noticing, Grandma slid the pan of cornbread in, propped the door closed, and lit a match to the wood in the other side. The fire caught and began to heat up the oven.

Before long a caterwauling started up that would have blinkied sweet milk.

Grandma kicked the prop to one side and the oven door slammed onto the linoleum with a bang that rattled the dishes. Cornbread batter up to his knees, Buttermilk leaped out and streaked up the stairs, yowling as he went.

In the middle of the ruckus, the doorbell rang.

Aunt Lila opened the door to a tall, blond man with a big friendly smile. Romeo Three had arrived.

"Welcome to West Virginia," she said. "Come on in and make yourself at home. I gotta look for a half-cooked cat."

He said he preferred his cat well done.

Aunt Lila looked up at him and busted out laughing.

We searched attic to cellar, following splats of batter upstairs and down, Charles Landwehr trailing along after Aunt Lila. Eventually we found Buttermilk under the bathtub, busy licking cornbread batter off his belly. Charles Landwehr reached back and scooped him out. Other than the long oval he'd scorched bald on one side, he didn't appear to have any damage. Mother said she didn't know how many lives that cat had left, but he'd sure as heck just used up one of them.

Grandma said she'd just as soon Mother didn't use words like heck. Mother rolled her eyes and headed to the kitchen to start a new batch of cornbread.

While Charles Landwehr and Aunt Lila cleaned up the batter Buttermilk had tracked through the house, Grandma went to fetch a jar of piccalilli from the fruit house, a cinderblock building that housed our stores of canned fruits and vegetables. Piccalilli is a golden relish of vegetables and fruit that goes just right with ham and most anything else you think to put it on.

Grandma didn't get far before she rushed back in, hollering for Grandpa.

"Come quick, Clev! He's got the butcher knife!"

Old man Dunkley, all crippled up with lumbago, was hobbling along in his yard trying to catch Granny Dunkley. They were our next-door neighbors. She hopped onto the cinderblock Grandpa had put next to her side of our fence, hitched her dress up and threw her leg over, barely able to reach the block on our side without impaling herself on the picket fence.

The old man hadn't managed to catch up yet.

Grandpa came out of our house holding a pop bottle of vinegar water left over from cleaning the windows. "Now Zeb, you put that knife down and go on back to the house." His voice was calm.

Old man Dunkley either couldn't hear him or didn't want to. The closer he got, the bigger that butcher knife looked.

"Zeb Dunkley, you stop or I'll be obliged to douse you with this poison," Grandpa said, a little louder this time. "Kill you deader than a rattlesnake. You'd be wise to quile yourself down."

The old man kept coming.

All of a sudden, Charles Landwehr leaped over the fence and grabbed the knife before the old man even realized what had happened. Disarmed and out of breath, the old man quieted right down. Charles Landwehr handed the knife to Granny Dunkley.

"I've a mind to poke a hole in that old man and let the meanness spill out of him," she said, "but I don't want it turning my grass yellow."

There was a mole on her chin I'd never paid any attention to, a great big one. She had tied a coarse black thread around it and finished it off with a bow, the ends of which hung down and waved back and forth when she talked. It was awful hard not to stare. About then Grandma came out with two plates of food she held on to until Charles Landwehr helped Granny Dunkley climb back over the fence.

"Come on, old man, let's go to the house and thank the good Lord for providing this fine supper," she said, starting down the path with the plates. "After you eat your fill, I'll read to you from the Good Book. Maybe some of it will sink in."

"Yes'm," he said, just meek as a mouse.

He tucked along behind her, following the tantalizing smells in her wake.

It was a peace that he would disturb again, but hopefully not that night.

After we ate supper, Mother went with Vonnie and me to check on the Dunkleys, taking strawberry shortcake as our excuse to visit. The old man was sitting in his favorite rocker smoking a pipe. Granny Dunkley sat opposite him on a mohair settee. She was smoking too, a homemade corncob pipe with a reed of some kind for the stem. They each smoked a pipe of applewood tobacco every evening after supper. The earthy sweetness that hung in the air lingered on me long after I went home.

Old man Dunkley's ponytailed hair and handlebar mustache made him look for all the world like Wild Bill Hickok, but it was Buffalo Bill he talked about all the time. He told tales of working in Buffalo Bill's Wild West Show, traveling around Colorado, and then going with the show to New York. He was old now, senile, my grandma said, and sometimes didn't know what he was talking about.

I believed every word he said.

"Be quiet, old man, these young'uns have heard enough of your yarns," Granny Dunkley said, going off to bring us a piece of the hard candy she kept in the icebox, one of several still in use on our street.

She reached up and loosened the string tied around the mole on her chin. "I expect this big old mole ought to be falling off before long," she said. "This string here's cutting off the blood to it." Holding both ends she pulled the knot a little tighter and retied the bow.

She held out two peppermint sticks for us to take. I noticed her long fingernails were yellowed and dirty. I'd wash the candy when I got home.

"I've got to keep candy hidden," she said, nodding in the old man's direction, "on account of he gets choked easy. I've got to keep an eye on him while he's eating it too." She handed him a piece of twisted peppermint. "Now you just suck on that, you hear?"

The candy was our signal to leave. It was time for the six o'clock news.

Like most everybody I knew, the Dunkleys never missed it.

The familiar voice of Gabriel Heatter came over the radio as the screen door banged closed behind us:

"Ah, there's good news tonight."

We went to bed before the chickens stopped squabbling, leaving Aunt Lila and Charles Landwehr in the front room talking and drinking a second pot of coffee. And that's where Grandma found them when she came downstairs the next morning. They'd talked the whole night through. She sent Aunt Lila upstairs to bed and Charles Landwehr to the guest room downstairs.

The Morning Glory Tourist Home was cancelled.

Charles Landwehr called his sister back in New Jersey to tell her he'd been invited to stay another week and he was taking us up on the offer.

"I'm having too much fun to leave now," I heard him say. "Here, they cook cats and chase each other with butcher knives— and the whole lot of them think they're normal."

It was a lightning-quick romance.

He proposed fast and Aunt Lila said yes fast. Grandpa asked if they were sure what they were getting themselves into.

"Absolutely not," Charles Landwehr replied, "but sometimes you have to take a deep breath and jump in the deep end."

Aunt Lila said she couldn't swim a lick, but she was jumping.

Grandma made the bride a blue-velvet suit to wear for the wedding, and Vonnie and I held boughs of greenery tied with strips of the blue velvet. Grandpa lent the groom a blue striped tie.

And so it happened that before the two week visit was up, Grandpa married Aunt Lila to Charles Landwehr in our back yard, autumn leaves drifting down on them like blessings.

There Be Dragons

The half-man, half-woman stood at the back of the stage. He or she, I wasn't sure which, wore a full skirt and a shirt and tie. I thought I noticed a slight swell of breasts. A dozen or so people milled around waiting for something, but I didn't know what. The men, coal miners most of them, wore overalls or blue jeans. They bent forward and hacked shards of blackened lungs into red bandanas to hide the blood. Their women, some holding children by the hand, wore pageboys and clean print dresses.

The carnival was in town, and Vonnie and I had talked Grandma into letting us go. We each got a dollar to spend, plus we'd broken our piggy bank and split another dollar and eighty-two cents. Grandma was still hanging in the car window giving my brother Hursey instructions as Grandpa pulled out of the driveway. This was the first time she'd let Hursey be in charge of us. He was sixteen, my sister, Vonnie, eleven, and I was nine.

As soon as Grandpa got out of sight, Hursey took off with his best friend, Billy Johnson, making us promise to meet them in an hour at the big beacon light that fanned over the town every night, beckoning people to come.

Madame Vadoma had set herself up near the entrance to the carnival, which was only a short piece down the hard road from the gypsy camp. Her "KNOWS ALL, SEES ALL, TELLS ALL" sign leaned against a table where she sat, long bony fingers splayed around a clear glass ball set in the middle. The gypsy man standing nearby sawed away at his violin, trying to drum up some business, but the people hurrying by hardly gave them a glance.

They'd probably seen the gypsies before.

Now they had a need for something new.

The barker called out to us. "Try your luck right here! Bust three balloons and take your pick from that bottom shelf for just one thin dime. Everybody wins and nobody loses. Come on over here, Blondie, win that kewpie doll you been eyeing."

Flush with money and raring to spend it, Vonnie tried for the kewpie doll with the curl on its forehead, but after spending thirty cents and only winning a paddle-ball and two kazoos, she gave up.

The man's eyes followed my sister as she walked away.

We stopped at the carousel and Vonnie climbed on a palomino that matched her hair, while I mounted a wild black steed with flashing red eyes. We scuffed through the sweet smelling sawdust to the refreshment stand and bought ten-cent hotdogs and pink cotton candy for another dime each, eating as we gawked up at the rusty old Ferris wheel. Although I wasn't too keen on the idea, I let Vonnie talk me into getting on it. The old wheel lurched and screeched up and up as riders were loaded into the swinging seats below. Just as we got to the top, it shook itself like a wet dog and stopped dead, holding us captive high above the midway while the operator cussed and kicked at the gunked-up machinery to get it started again. Vonnie, who tended toward a nervous stomach, began to heave. I told her to stick her head over the side, and she did, just in time to puke up pink cotton candy. I didn't see where the throw-up landed, but I imagined it splatting down all warm and gooey on somebody's bald head. When I told her that, she heaved again, and a froth of pink bubbles came out of her nose. I laughed and she got so mad she didn't speak to me until I bought her a bottle of RC pop to settle her stomach down.

The music from the calliope trailed us down the midway as we hurried to meet the guys at the beacon, but they were nowhere to be seen. We walked on past the little kids' Merry-Go-Round and pony rides. Past the Tilt-A-Whirl and the Bullet. Past the balloon game and shooting game and ring game. We ended up at the far end of the midway where most of the side shows were set up.

Grandma had warned us those places were just as crooked as a rattlesnake and we had no business whatsoever going anywhere near them and she'd better not hear tell that we had or we would be plenty sorry and we should mark her words because we'd have her to deal with when we got home and make no mistake about that.

So that's where we headed.

We walked past gaudy signs advertising the Fun House and Freaks of Nature and the Tunnel of Love before Vonnie spotted Hursey and Billy standing in front of a rickety stage gazing up at hoochie-coochie girls. The sign overhead said "Ooh La La Ladies, Fresh from Paris, France." The women wore skimpy skirts and fishnet stockings with holes in them and sequined halters on top. They had painted their shoes with gilt, black streaks showing through the brush marks on their skint-up high heels. Puckering their lips and making kissy sounds, they gyrated to music that thrummed through big loudspeakers that crackled and buzzed. One girl tapped to the front and did a routine to "Chattanooga Shoeshine Boy," spreading a mouth smeared with red lipstick in the direction of the men, her tongue licking out around bad teeth.

The record got stuck on "choo-choo," repeating it over and over.

The bad-teeth girl kept right on dancing to the "choo-choo choo-choo choo-choo" and pretty soon the men were egging her on.

The barker, sensing the excitement, shooed the girls into the tent behind the stage and began his pitch. "You ain't seen nuthin' yet. Come on inside where the real show is about to begin. It's gonna be the best two bits you're ever gonna spend. Yes sirree, you'll be down on your knees thankin' me, and that's no lie. Last call, gentlemen, show's gonna start in two minutes."

The men and boys swiveled their heads as they snaked hands into pockets to fish out a quarter. Seeing hoochie-coochie girls wasn't anything I was interested in when I could see a real live alligator man and a two-headed chicken right down the midway. Hursey bought tickets for him and Billy, making me pinky swear I'd never tell. And I wouldn't, because that would be the end of us ever going anywhere with him again.

My brother and sister were always saying I was dumb, but I wasn't that dumb.

Vonnie and I bought cherry snow cones piled high with ice and drenched with sticky red syrup that dripped onto our shoes. We spent what was left of our money to buy tickets to the Oddities of the World freak show which promised not only the alligator man and the two-headed chicken, but a half-man, half-woman, who was pictured on one of the huge, hand-painted posters hanging behind the stage. The painting showed a figure that was split down the middle from top to bottom, one half of it a man and the other half a woman, with words that said:

SEE A GREEK MYTH COME TO LIFE
HERMAPHRODITE
GOD AND GODDESS IN ONE BODY

Holding hands tight, Vonnie and I walked down boards laid for a ramp into the tent. A huge woman lolled in a chair, her natural bulk made bigger by horsehair padding you could see a little of poking out of her sleeves. Sweat teared down her face, washing tracks through her makeup. Her hand, white and bloated as a dead fish, waved back and forth.

The two-headed chicken walking around in a cage and the scaly alligator man both looked real enough to me, but I didn't know how to tell if the coal black figure stretched out in a coffin was a genuine petrified man.

A midget dressed in a red and yellow checkered clown suit ran around in the audience doing handstands. Sometimes he bent down and looked up the women's dresses, honking a horn and covering his eyes every time he did it. One woman squealed while another cussed at him and kicked him in the knee. He laughed and pretended it didn't hurt.

The man-woman walked to the front of the stage, keeping its face turned toward the naked bulb that hung from a cord in the center of the tent. It lifted its skirt to expose a fingerling of pink flesh dangling from a furry nest. A flash, then the skirt dropped. When it spun around and walked away, a sign on its back declared, "I AM NOT RESPONSIBLE FOR WHAT I AM."

A few hoots and catcalls started up and died away.

Vonnie and I turned and clambered back up the ramp as fast as we could, the uneven boards bouncing under our feet. I stumbled and fell, Vonnie still clutching my hand and dragging me along before I regained my footing. I hadn't even felt the splinter pierce my knee, but when she pulled it out, bright red blood and cherry snow cone juice mingled on my white Easter shoes and anklets.

Hursey gave the kewpie doll he won at the carnival to Vonnie so she wouldn't tattle to Grandma about the hoochie-coochie girls, and he talked Billy into giving me a yoyo, for the same reason, I suspected. He gave Grandma a green glass bowl. She served potato salad in it that night and from then on.

I'd always believed Grandma had eyes in the back of her head. Like the portraits of ancestors hanging on our walls, her eyes seemed to follow me all the time. I convinced myself she could see right through my sorry skin and bones to every sin I had hidden deep in my darkest corners.

Like the time Lohny Pemberton tried to get me to pull my underpants down.

Although I knew it was wrong, I might have done it anyway just to show off the lavender ones I had on, the ones with Thursday on them, but it was Friday and Lohny would say I was dumb for wearing the wrong day. But I'd done it on purpose. The Thursday ones were my favorite color so I'd worn them two days straight, putting the clean Friday ones in the laundry hamper so Grandma wouldn't catch on. Somebody came out of the house and let the screen door bang shut. Grandma hollered after them to not be letting that door slam and Lohny took off like he got shot. And he might have if Grandpa had known what he was up to.

I had a bunch more sins to worry about.

I'd rolled dried corn tassels in a piece of dampened husk and smoked the pretend cigarettes, coughing and hacking at the harsh scrape of smoke in my windpipe. Sometimes Sissy and I stayed up all night gambling with real playing cards. I'd lied when I didn't need to, claiming I'd already brushed my teeth instead of saying I was fixing to. When I spilled Vonnie's Blue Waltz perfume, I denied knowing a thing about it even though Uncle Ed, who'd served in France during World War I and had a picture of himself in Paris with a French girl to prove it, said the whole house stunk like a French whorehouse. Grandma said she wouldn't allow him to be a corrupting influence.

But I was already corrupt.

My face flushed every time I thought about what I'd seen at the carnival, and I thought about it most of the time. To tell the truth, I worried myself sick about the particulars of that peculiar body. Was it called a he or a she? How did it sound when it talked? Would it have a husband or a wife? Would it be a mommy or a daddy? Which bathroom did it use?

I still called the man-woman *it* in my head.

Although I knew in my heart that was wrong, I didn't know what was right. Grandma might know, but I couldn't ask without telling on myself, and Vonnie refused to talk about it at all. Thinking about it made me uneasy, so I decided to put it out of my mind, and for the most part that worked. An occasional image resurfaced, not of what I'd seen, but of something else, some disturbing thing I could not name. Confusion and shame and a vague sadness writhed in me like a tangle of fishing worms.

From my bed I watched the beacon wag an accusing finger across the dark heavens outside my bedroom window. I got on my knees and said, "Now I lay me down to sleep I pray the Lord my soul to keep if I should die before I wake I pray the Lord my soul to take. Amen."

I had crossed some line that was invisible, and it was too late to turn back.

A picture in my brother's geography book showed a map of the world in ancient days. There were known countries and continents—the rest of the map had the words *BEYOND THERE BE DRAGONS.*

There was no warning sign, no caution light, no line drawn in the sand.

I had wandered into dragon territory.

Mr. Pursley's World

Grandma didn't know about the carnival sideshow, but she still noticed I was acting a little mopey. Vonnie too. That wasn't like us at all.

"Piano lessons!" Grandma announced, after luring me and Vonnie and Mother to the table for just-baked molasses cookies. "It's high time these girls had piano lessons. They need something to get them out of the doldrums, and I expect that's just the thing to do it." Grandma said if Mother bought the piano, she'd finance the lessons from her butter-and-egg money.

Although I campaigned hard for dancing lessons, Grandma wouldn't hear of it. "You don't need to be wringing and twisting around calling unnecessary attention to yourself."

"How come playing the piano isn't calling attention?"

"That's a cat of a different color. You'd be playing for the glory of the Lord."

No matter how I pleaded my case, she could not be persuaded. Grandma most likely had visions of me and Vonnie playing duets at Sunday services, her nodding up at us from the front row. "My oh my, Sister Cales, that was a fine rendition of 'Whispering Hope,'" the church ladies would say. Mother shopped the classified ads in the *Raleigh Register* until she spotted a Baldwin upright advertised cheap. When it took its place at the far end of the dining room, even our untrained ears could tell it needed work, so she found a man to come tune it.

When he saw our piano, he let out a whistle. "That's a mighty fine piano you got yourself. You gals been playing any piano rolls?"

"No sir, not a one," I answered, although I didn't have the faintest notion what a piano roll was.

"Well, I'm going to show you how to play this piano without ever taking a lesson. But you'll have to wait until I finish the tuning, and it's sounding like that could take a fair amount of time."

We watched him plunge his arms deep into the works of the piano, fiddling with pins and strings and tuning hammer until each key sounded perfect.

When he finished, he called us over.

"You got yourselves a player piano," he said, sliding two small panels back to reveal a hidden compartment. "Stick a piano roll in there and the song will play itself as long as you keep pumping them big pedals. They's a bunch of rolls in the bench—let's load her up and see how she sounds."

The man clicked a roll in place. As he pumped, "Tea for Two" played, the keys moving up and down without anybody touching them.

We had us a magical piano, and I couldn't wait to show it off.

"I can't play a lick with you staring so hard it's boring a hole in my back," I said to Sissy. "Turn the other way, but first pinky swear cross your heart you won't peek."

She gave me a look that meant she'd do it, but she wouldn't like it. Although we were best friends, I knew she was getting tired of me bossing her, so I started playing the minute she turned her back. I didn't want to lose my audience. Stretching my legs to reach, I pedaled hard, managing to play "You are My Sunshine" all the way through without a hitch.

"How'd you learn that so good?" Previous dealings with me had led to her suspicious nature.

"It's playing by ear," I told her. "At least that's what Grandma calls it. That's when you hear something once and sit down and play it good as it sounds on the radio. Soon as I sat down I started playing songs front to finish just as pretty as you please."

Grandpa called that a gift-wrapped lie. He was against lying in all its forms, but he thought a half-lie was about the worst kind. Folks, he said, didn't expect to find a lie in the middle when you wrapped it up in the truth and tied a big red bow on it.

It was the kind of lying I did best.

I got away with it several times before Sissy broke her vow not to look and caught me red-handed changing the piano roll. It was quite a while before she believed a word I said.

And I didn't believe her pinky-swear-cross-your-heart promise either.

Mr. Pursley, who lived on the second floor of a fancy house on Woodlawn Avenue, came highly recommended, so Mother took us to meet him and make arrangements for lessons. Holding his hand out, palm down and fingers extended, he looked more like he expected my mother to kiss his hand than shake it.

He offered her the chair to his right and motioned me and Vonnie to a small settee, while he arranged his slim body on the tapestry fainting couch. I fought to keep myself from brushing the city bus off my behind before sullying the needlepointed tapestry I was about to sit on. Glad I had on my best Sunday dress, I tugged it over my scabby knees.

"I've prepared a light tea," he said. "You and the young ladies must join me."

Heels barely touching the floor, he glided out, reappearing in a few minutes balancing a tray laden with a silver teapot and china cups as thin as painted eggshells.

Mr. Pursley leaned forward. "Would you care for a watercress sandwich? And a petit four, perhaps?"

I had always taken my chances with food, so I took one of each.

Mr. Pursley leaned a little more toward Mother. "If I may, I have a few questions regarding the young ladies' lessons."

Mr. Pursley wanted to know what day and what time and how long the lessons would be and would we come to his studio or prefer he come to our home and by the way did we have a piano suitable for practice? It was decided we would go to his studio every Wednesday afternoon from five to six for one half hour each, and yes, we certainly did have a piano suitable for practice—then, and only then, Mr. Pursley accepted us as students.

And so began our foray into Mr. Pursley's world.

Each week Mother sipped cups of oolong tea in the parlor while he played for us before we began lessons. Hands arched over the keyboard with the tension of a small animal set to strike, he announced the piece and the composer before he began. The opening of "Tchaikovsky's Piano Concerto No. 1" filled the room— soft slow, louder faster, soft again. Then, as the crescendo built, his fingers blistered over the keyboard, his eyes closed, and perspiration misted his upper lip.

One day Mr. Pursley told Mother we were to perform at his annual recital concert at Memorial Hall. He never asked if we wanted to be in it. To be fair, he never said we had to either. It didn't matter. There was no getting around it with Mother and Grandma all atwitter.

It rained a gully washer on recital day, threatening to ruin the dress Grandma made me from a silk World War II parachute Mother ordered cheap from the back of a magazine. She made Vonnie a parachute dress too. Then she made bedspreads for every bed in the house with some of the leftover silk. When I sat on my parachute bedspread in my parachute dress, I almost disappeared.

By evening it had almost rained itself out, so we arrived only a little damp and a little late. When it was my turn, I walked across the stage beaming my best Lana Turner smile. Not watching where I was going, I tripped and fell flat, catching my heel and ripping my new dress. Although I didn't break anything, my pride was bruised to the bone. I made it through my piece, but my heart wasn't in it. I wanted to go home. I wanted to cry. I wanted to start all over.

But most of all, I wanted to play in another concert.

And next time I wouldn't fall on my behind.

Grandma got it into her head that if we could play good enough to be in a concert, we could assuredly accompany her and Grandpa singing a duet for Sunday services. The fact that she could not sing a lick was just a bothersome detail she felt she could overcome with practice and the help of the Lord. And if Grandma thought Grandpa could sing, well then, he would just have to oblige her.

She borrowed one of the red hymnals from church and sat at the kitchen table leafing through to find the right hymn, finally deciding on "Amazing Grace" because it didn't have too many highs and lows. We each learned our part, Vonnie on the bass and me on the treble, but for the life of us we couldn't put the two together. We would get a few notes in and I'd be going too fast or she'd hold the half note too long or we'd find some other way to mess up.

Grandma determined one or the other of us would have to play both parts.

Vonnie backed out, but I was getting a little taste of show business and liked it. Every evening I plunked and plinked until I got a barely recognizable rendition of "Amazing Grace" going. Grandma managed to hit a good note every now and again, and Grandpa did his best to sing bass, but truth be told, they sounded awful. And while we're truth-telling, so did I.

Before we took the show on the road, Grandma decided to hold a rehearsal. Sister Wood was at the house visiting, and so was Sissy, and we recruited Mother and Aunt Lila and Vonnie from the kitchen where they were making crepe-paper flowers to take to the cemetery for Decoration Day. Red bandanas tied around their heads Rosie the Riveter style, Mother and Aunt Lila came in and sat cross-legged on the floor, still rubbing at crepe-paper stains on their fingers. Vonnie tagged along behind, wearing a bandana like theirs.

We had our audience.

We managed to start pretty even, me playing and grinning and Grandma opening wide and warbling toward the ceiling. As for Grandpa, he had his mouth twisted peculiar, trying to reach the bass notes. It didn't matter, me and Grandma drowned him out anyway. I expect Grandma thought we'd get better as the rehearsal went on, but I was tired and had slowed down like a music box needing a wind-up.

"Well now, wasn't that something?" Sister Wood asked.

Mother and Aunt Lila agreed that yes, it most certainly was. Vonnie and Sissy had enough sense to keep quiet, that is, until Grandma made the mistake of asking them how they thought we did.

Sissy smiled and nodded and got away without saying.

But Vonnie didn't hold back.

"I'll tell you one thing right now," she blurted. "I'm not setting a foot in that church again if y'all get up there doing that in front of God and everybody else that knows us."

Grandma said she expected it didn't sound that bad, but when nobody came to her defense, she said of course everybody knew this was just a rehearsal and all. We practiced a couple more times, but soon Grandma stopped mentioning it and switched to a project she was good at—making quilts for the missionaries in Africa.

But I wasn't ready to call it quits. Mr. Pursley's next recital was scheduled for the following month, and I was counting on redeeming myself.

When he came up with the idea of me and Vonnie playing a duet, I could not be talked into it. This was my moment, and I wasn't about to share it. I finally decided on "Leibestraum," which was a good bit harder than anything I'd tried before. I was determined to shine, so I practiced that song until everybody at home was sick to death of it.

By the day of the concert, I was ready.

My taffeta skirt rustled as I went wringing and twisting up the steps, crossed over to the piano and flashed my toothiest movie-star smile at my audience. I sat down, arranged the taffeta around me, and played "Leibestraum" through to the end. After I took my bow, I walked off the stage just a little slower than necessary. Like the last square of Hershey's chocolate on your tongue, some things are meant to be savored.

Although I never played in public again, I had done what I set out to do. By this time Vonnie and I were bored with the piano, so we talked Mother into letting us quit taking lessons. Still, anytime I hear the opening movement of a Tchaikovsky concerto, Mr. Pursley is playing piano in his parlor, and I am sipping tea from china I could crush in my hand like a Dixie Cup.

24

The River Ran Cold

I watched the top half of Vonnie streak by the window. Mother, waving a cherry-tree switch in her hand, sprinted a few steps behind. By the time they came around again, I could tell Mother was gaining on her. I figured it would take a couple more laps before Vonnie got caught.

"Save me, Grandpa, save me!" she hollered, but he was off somewhere out of earshot.

Grandma didn't even look up. "What must the neighbors think?" she muttered, darning away at a sizable hole in a thin black sock, more than likely one Grandpa needed for church.

Vonnie had settled in on pitching fits to get her way—and Mother had settled in on not letting her. It all started when Mother hung her new stockings out to dry after rinsing them in vinegar water, which was supposed to make them last longer, although I don't know if it did.

"Vonnie, run quick and get my hose off the line before it rains," she directed.

Though the sky was cloudless, thunder rumbled under its breath nearby. Just as Vonnie got to the clothesline, rain began to plop on the ground. She yanked the stockings off and ran for the house.

And Mother saw her do it.

She lit in about those being brand-new stockings bought special to go with the suit she was wearing that very night and she'd be unlikely to find that color again, not to mention how she'd ever afford to buy another pair even if she did. Why Vonnie had snatched them off the line and ruined them was a complete mystery. It wasn't because she didn't know better, because she certainly did, and there was no need to say she didn't.

Mother examined the stockings toe to thigh, sticking her hand up each one and holding it to the light.

There was a snag in the foot of the second stocking.

Instead of keeping her mouth shut like any reasonable person would know to do, my sister talked back. The more Mother fussed and fumed, the more Vonnie sassed. She was bound and determined to get in the last word, but Mother wasn't about to let her. That soon led to Vonnie being sent to break a switch off the cherry tree. Vonnie handed her the switch, then took off running.

I was almost rooting for her.

There's things about a person you can't help but admire.

The rain petered out after only a spit and a promise. I went out and sat on the porch steps so I'd have a ringside seat for the final round. Mother held Vonnie's wrist with one hand, trying and mostly failing to land a swipe or two on her twisting legs. Knowing full well she wouldn't get switched while she was down, Vonnie collapsed belly-up on the grass like Queenie did when she came upon a bad-tempered cur. She sucked in some air, arched her back, and screamed bloody murder.

Grandma had heard enough. She came out of the house, a cup in her hand, making a beeline for the middle of the fracas.

"Young lady, you'd best stop that racket by the time I count to three or I'll douse you so fast it'll make your head swim, and don't you think for one minute I won't."

She lifted the cup higher. "One. Two. Three."

Vonnie, still squalling, flashed her eyes at Grandma to determine if she was serious.

She determined wrong.

Before a heartbeat passed, Grandma dumped the cup of water on Vonnie, who sputtered and coughed and made a big show of it

like she was strangling to death. Grandma didn't fall for it. Without
a word, she handed Vonnie the dishtowel she usually wore thrown
over her shoulder. All the starch taken out of her, Vonnie sopped at
her hair and tears and runny nose.

"Come on to the house now and get you some supper while it's
hot," Grandma said, talking just as nice as you please. "It's ten past
the hour, so we'll have to hurry a little."

She held out her hand and Vonnie took it.

Miraculously, the fit was over.

Mother and Vonnie appeared to be past their fuss about the
stockings, and dinner went off without a hitch. Grandma saw to that.
Every meal we sat down together—breakfast at seven, dinner at noon,
and supper at six, folding our white flour-sack napkins and placing
them on our chairs after each meal. After supper Grandma collected
them and put clean ones out before breakfast the next morning.

"Tuck that napkin in before you drip all over yourself,"
Grandma scolded. "Your mother's expecting company in a little bit
and you need to be presentable."

I picked up an ear of buttered corn, but not before I took the
napkin off my lap and tucked it in the front of my dress.

Oh, we had rules up to the elbows we weren't supposed to put
on the table.

"Vonnie, Vonnie, if you're able, get your elbows off the table," I
singsonged. Then she watched extra hard to try to catch me.

Grandma'd say things like: "Wait till Grandpa says grace."
"Don't talk with your mouth full." "Say, 'Please pass the gravy,'
instead of doing a boardinghouse reach." "Ask if you can be
excused before you up and leave." "Consider what's fit to talk about
at the table lest you go blurting something out."

She looked straight at me when she said that blurting part.

"I think I've heard enough of that," she'd say, drawing her eyebrows down and giving me a look.

I didn't seem to have an ear for what was fit talk, but I could
depend on Grandma to set me straight. David Stanley getting his

nose bloodied wasn't fit, although it wasn't a fair fight since the other boy was way older. David, on the other hand, was wiry and tough and had stood his ground, so I was rooting for him until the very end. Nor was Sissy peeing her pants in class, making a perfect round puddle under her desk. She'd raised her hand like we were supposed to and the teacher paid her no mind at all so it wasn't her fault. And Cora Hinkley coming to school with her hair chopped off because she had head lice couldn't be talked about. The teacher forced her to wear a cap made from cutting off an old stocking. That just seemed wrong. I wanted to see if Grandma agreed with me, but she was hurrying us through a supper of macaroni and cheese, green beans with scrappy ham, apple dumplings, and cornbread left over from dinner. She was anxious to get the kitchen cleaned up before Mother's company came at seven.

Mother had got a notion to take up the wool cabbage-rose carpet, uncovering oak floors dulled by time. She'd have the carpet cut and bound into throw rugs. Although she usually tackled such jobs herself, she decided the job was big enough to call in a professional. Ralph Matthews, listed in the Yellow Pages as owner and operator of the Tru Finish Floor Company, showed up.

After the job was done, he called our house several times. Grandma answered every time.

Had he left his hat there?

No, she was sure he hadn't.

Had she come across that hat?

No, it was nowhere to be found.

Finally he called and Mother answered.

That's when he asked her for a date.

Mother spent a long time getting herself ready, putting on the soft gray herringbone suit and white crepe blouse she'd pressed earlier. Dabbed with clear nail polish so it wouldn't run, the snag in her taupe hose was covered by her black spike pumps. She clipped pearl earrings to her ears and finished the look off with a red hat topped by a tuft of feathers.

Ralph, a confirmed bachelor who lived a mile or so away
with his mother, was blond and good-looking. I guess that was my
mother's type, because my father was blond and good-looking too.
Mother and Ralph saw each other regularly after that first date.
His mother didn't seem happy about it. Grandma probably wasn't
either, although I never heard her say so. It didn't matter. He was at
our house most every evening.

Ralph owned a summer camp on the Greenbrier River, not far
from where Grandpa held the baptisms in water that ran cold and
deep. Sometimes when we went to Ralph's place on the river, I'd
think of Grandpa standing in a suit in that numbing water, a few
converts waiting their turn. People on the bank sang,

> There is a fountain filled with blood,
> drawn from Emmanuel's veins,
> and sinners plunged beneath that flood
> lose all their guilty stains,
> lose all their guilty stains.

Images played in my head like a moving picture show.

The summer camp wasn't a camp at all; it was actually a frame
house. A big room across the front held a dilapidated divan and
several beds, and one end had been partitioned off to make a separate
bedroom. The enclosed back porch was now a kitchen with an old
Frigidaire, the kind with the motor poking up through the top, and
an oilcloth-covered picnic table. Some of the back porch had been
sectioned off to put in a bathroom that opened into the big front room.
Next to the house, a weathered rowboat lay upturned against the trunk
of a massive tree that leaned so low over the river we could walk out on
the trunk. Vonnie and I spread a towel and ate our lunchmeat sandwiches there, balancing cold bottles of Dr Pepper between our legs.
We ate strange foods like pickle loaf, baloney, liverwurst, sliced white
bread, and Little Debbie oatmeal cakes.

Grandma didn't think that stuff was fit to eat.

Ralph painted KATY'S FIRST YACHT on both sides of the
boat in wavy blue letters that ran front to back. My mother's name

was Kathleen, but Ralph called her Katy from the start. When he put the boat in the water, he broke half a bottle of ginger ale on the front for good luck. Mother wouldn't let him waste the whole bottle. Although he'd patched up the bottom of the boat until it looked like a crazy quilt, the river still seeped in. Every now and then Vonnie and I bailed with an old coffee can we kept fishing worms in. After a few trips, Ralph came up with the idea of tethering the boat to a tree and leaving it in the water. That made the wood swell up so it didn't leak as bad.

While Vonnie and I splashed in the river, Mother sat on a quilt rubbing suntan lotion made of baby oil and iodine on her legs. Vonnie laid back until her whole body was under water except her face. She held her arms out and floated, toes just breaking the surface. She was showing off, so I ignored her. Mother had sent her for swimming lessons at Waterdale, the community pool near downtown. She promised me I'd be big enough next summer.

I stuck my toe in, gradually wading up to my knees. The cold always took me by surprise. Fed by icy mountain streams, the rivers and lakes never warmed up, no matter how hot the summer. Buttery yellow clay oozed between my toes. Silver fish no more than an inch long nibbled at tiny air bubbles on my ankles. I hopped from one leg to the other to keep them away. I imagined crawdads waiting to grab hold of my toe, but I'd stirred the water up too much to see them. The seat of my bathing suit, a green checkered one of Vonnie's I hadn't quite grown into, filled with silt. Holding the elastic out and wriggling my bottom back and forth under water helped, but I was still gritty.

Naked as baby mice, Vonnie and I hurried to spray each other down before the hose, warmed like a coiled snake in the summer sun, ran cold again. Teeth chattering, we wrapped chenille housecoats around us. We thawed out on a quilt that smelled of mothballs and fell asleep to the river slurping at the muddy bank.

Ralph was just back from picking up the Sunday paper.

"Fellow at the filling station told me there's something down the river we need to see before we head back," he said to Mother.

"This is likely our last boat trip this summer, so pack up a picnic and we'll make a day of it."

We loaded the boat up to the gills, making it ride low in the water. Ralph paddled down the river a piece and around the bend. There, not a mile from our place, a swinging bridge swagged over a narrow place in the river.

"Can we walk on it?" I asked Ralph, sure the answer would be no.

"I don't see why not," he said, "that is, if it's okay with your mother."

Ralph tied the boat off, and we walked over to examine the bridge, which hung ten feet or so above the water. Truth be told, it looked downright shoddy up close. The ropes were grayed and stiff. Some of the boards were missing or rotted through. I didn't want to step a foot on it, but I couldn't back out now.

Ralph started over first, with me, Vonnie, and Mother following close behind.

The bridge was narrow enough to hold on to the ropes on both sides. It swayed and creaked as we walked, scarier than any rust-scaled ride I'd been on at the carnival. Vonnie, who wasn't a fraidy-cat like me, leaned over the side to look down at the water. The ropes groaned as the bridge tilted to a dizzying slant.

"Quit doing that!" I complained. "You're gonna make me fall."

But it was too late. My foot slipped and one leg plunged through a space between the boards. I tried, but I couldn't get my leg out of that hole. Ralph and Mother each held to a side rope with one hand and pulled me straight up with the other. My leg was scraped from the knee down, but I wasn't about to cry and have Vonnie call me a bawl-baby all day long.

Ralph built a fire from dead wood we gathered along the bank. He whittled a few green branches to a point, sticking them in the river to soak before we speared weenies to roast for hotdogs. Mother stirred ketchup and brown sugar into cans of beans she heated on the coals at the edge of the fire. We poked marshmallows on the sticks six at a time and charred them black in the fire. Then we pulled the burnt part off and toasted the gooey part black again.

After we splashed the stickiness off, we begged to play in the river, but Mother said we had to wait an hour so we wouldn't get cramps. We passed the time by fishing and soon had a whole string of trout. I'd never caught more than a minnow or a crawdad, but Vonnie claimed she'd caught lots of fish before. If she had, I'd sure never seen them. Ralph poured water on the fire and tidied up while Mother tended to my scraped leg, feeling around for splinters. Vonnie started paddling around on one of the inner tubes we'd dragged along behind the boat.

The cries come from a distance.

We look up and see Vonnie halfway across the river, her inner tube nowhere in sight.

Ralph takes off running, thrashing through the shallows until the water is deep enough to swim. Mother and I stand and watch.

Vonnie's head goes under, an arm trailing down.

Everything is in slow motion.

She comes back up, hair tangled over her face, then sinks again. By my count she's going down for the third time when Ralph reaches for her. She gets a stranglehold around his neck, but he grips both her hands and turns her to the side before she can pull him under. He swims with one arm, holding her head above water with the other. His arm crooks, dips in and pulls back, but slowly, like the wounded wing of a bird. I want him to swim faster.

Lord don't let my sister die Lord don't let my sister die Lord don't let my sister die, repeats over and over in my head. Ever now and then I add, *I am sorry for all the times I've been mean to her.* And I mean it. I hope God believes me.

Ralph carries Vonnie to shore and lays her on her stomach, head to the side. Coughing and gagging, she retches up a mouthful of river water.

But that's a relief.

It means she's breathing, although a bit unevenly at first. Hands shaking, he turns her over to check her eyes. They are bloodshot, but she sees him, knows where she is. Mother rubs her with towels we'd brought and wraps her in a quilt. She starts to pink-up some. The first thing she wants is for somebody to find her inner tube.

I helped Ralph clean the trout on a log when we got back to the camp house. He chopped off their heads and split them down their bellies, stripping out the guts and throwing them downstream for the turtles and crawdads to eat. Mother dredged the fish in corn-meal and browned them in lard. Everything was packed up, so she covered the picnic table with layers of the morning newspaper and laid the fish there to drain, frying up cornbread fritters in the same skillet. We ate in silence, tearing the fish off the bones with our fingers. We never talked about what happened. I knew there were people who would have. But not us.

Grandpa and I are at the river. The sky is silvered, the sun a dull orange ball. Tree leaves tremble over stilled green water. No squirrels chatter, no crows caw, no mosquitoes buzz near my ear. There is only the silence. He lowers a young girl under the water. Her hair, long and straight, floats to the top. Her eyes are wide open, but I can't make out her face. As Grandpa lifts her up, water flows down her body. Her arms twine above her head. She's not a girl anymore. She's a marble fountain.

When the water turns to blood I wake up.

I don't tell anybody about the dream.

I never knew that dreams could come back and repeat themselves, but this one did. On those mornings, after being startled awake, my breath caught in my throat until I saw Vonnie asleep next to me, hair spread over her rumpled pillow, one pajamaed leg on top of the covers. Then I'd look for the pulse in her throat. I was nicer to her on days after the dream.

Vonnie and I never once talked about her almost drowning at the river. I don't believe Grandma ever knew about it—Mother wouldn't have wanted her to worry. Like everything else in my life that needed talking about, I kept the dream to myself. I remembered when I saw the man/woman at the carnival sideshow and how disturbing the images were when they came back in my mind. I had decided back then to put them out of my head by thinking about good things instead. And I did.

I decided to try that with the dream. Before I went to sleep I would think of all the good things I could dream about. It took longer, but the dream did go away. After that, there was a freedom I'd not experienced before. I had discovered a power I never knew I had. I didn't quite know what to make of it. But I knew there were choices I could make deep inside myself. And I knew my life would be made of those choices.

Grandma saw our red dog road as a place where I might fall down and get hurt.

But I knew if I did, I'd get back up.

And that red dog road would lead me to every place I would ever go in my lifetime.

25

The Mountain
Fell Away

Flapjack plodded around the circle, lifting his tail from time to time to spew a stream of steamy gas and partially digested cane into the air. It was my job to fill the wheelbarrow with sawdust and dump a shovelful on the piles and puddles that fell on the old mule's path. Every time he passed he gave me the evil eye, like I was the one that stunk worse than a polecat. I held my nose with one hand and tried to shovel with the other. I didn't last long on the job.

Grandma and Mother and I were at my Uncle Vertis's place in Daniels, a town no more than a wide place in the road, and we'd brought Sissy along. We were going to make molasses. We were promised a picnic supper at the pines after the work was done. It was a magical place, a forest where long-needled pines soared so high they sometimes pierced the pale underbelly of the clouds. Years of fallen needles squelched the life out of most of the saplings and undergrowth that tried to take hold, but wood ferns grew in places, and chartreuse and lavender lichens spread lacy doilies over the trunks of fallen trees. Something drew me to that place. Maybe it was the quiet, which was so deep I felt angels hovering nearby, or fairies. Uncle Vertis said he'd put a swing up there, but that was a couple summers ago and I hadn't seen hide nor hair of one yet.

The molasses making was set up in the front yard, where Flapjack was harnessed to a contraption Uncle Vertis had put together to feed the sorghum cane through. It was attached to a wooden trough that angled into a kettle to catch the squeezings, a thin trickle of juice we boiled down to make molasses.

Uncle Vertis kept the fire going and fed the stalks of cane into the machine, while the women took turns gathering the frothy green scum from the syrup with a long skimmer paddle. The skimmings would go into the hog slop that evening. Once the syrup boiled down, it was cooled and poured into mason jars and sealed. If you boiled the squeezings three times, you got blackstrap, which was darker and not so sweet as the first boilings. Blackstrap was Grandpa's favorite. I pretended I liked it best.

When Uncle Vertis took his shirt off, he exposed a barrel chest furred over with springy black hair. He got that from Grandpa's side, but his hawk nose and high cheekbones made a strong showing of the bronzed Cherokee blood carried from a few generations back on Grandma's side of the family. Put a feather headdress on him and he could have posed as an Indian chief. Uncle Vertis, who knew lots of stuff about West Virginia history, said the Cherokee were all over the mountains around Beckley in years past.

Aunt Nalda said for Uncle Vertis to get a shirt on in front of his mother for goodness' sake, he was raised to know better than going around half naked. He answered, something I didn't quite catch, but he pulled his shirt back on, leaving it partway unbuttoned in protest.

"You better watch your mouth in front of these children or I'll wash it out with soap," Grandma scolded, so she must have heard him cuss, but her words to him never had teeth. I didn't see why, but there was no getting around it. It was the boys in the family Grandma doted on.

When Uncle Vertis walked into the room, her eyes lit up. "Excuse my French," he'd say, but it wouldn't be long before he'd let another cussword rip. Grandma would light into him for taking the Lord's name in vain and he'd say he was sorry and try to be better for a while, but not for long. Vonnie and I called him Uncle Dirty. Grandma didn't like that, but she hoped it would shame him into changing his ways.

I thought he was perfect.

Boo Boudreaux drove into Uncle Vertis's yard, bringing his car and our molasses making to a stop. Uncle Vertis walked over to talk to him out of earshot of Grandma. Slick as quicksilver, Boo slid through the window feet first and loped the few steps back to open the trunk. He wore his black hair tied with a bandana, his pencil mustache and goatee not hiding a thin scar that hooked from the top of his ear through his upper lip. One of the neighbors told Aunt Nalda he was a Cajun from Louisiana, and his given name was Champagne or maybe Champlain. Some thought that was too hifalutin' for a moonshiner, so they'd started calling him Boo. A licorice whip of a man, he didn't seem to be much given to idle talk or foolishness.

Digging under a hodgepodge of newspapers, tools, a dirty doll baby, and a pile of hunting clothes, he unearthed a paper sack with the top twisted closed.

"Get caught up with what I owe you next time," Uncle Vertis said, taking the sack.

"Ain't gonna *be* no next time until you do," Boo told him, nodding his respect to the women in the yard as he swung back through the car window.

Boo jammed the gearshift into reverse and stomped on the gas. The tires dug deep into the soft ground before the wheels caught and the car backed out, taking off like it was running from the law.

It probably was.

Uncle Vertis whistled under his breath as Boo fishtailed down the road. "That boy's got hisself on the growling end," he said to nobody in particular. "Looks like he's not scared of it neither."

He watched Boo disappear in a cloud of dust and smoke.

Although Uncle Vertis was one of the smartest people I knew, he never seemed to get ahead. He worked in the mines here and there, off and on, just managing to make enough to keep the lights on and do what he wanted—and that was to have enough in his pocket to buy junked cars and junked parts to fix them up, with enough change left over for a jar of moonshine every now and then.

Uncle Vertis had uncommon ability when it came to machines. He made some money at it, fixing people's broke-down cars and trucks and tractors and selling others he bought cheap and got going again. He'd got hold of a sprayer somewhere and made more money painting those same cars and trucks and tractors.

He'd once driven up to our house in a many-colored automobile he'd put together from scraps from the junkyard. When Grandma asked what kind of car it was, he laughed and said it was a genuine one of a kind Calesmobile, calling it after his own last name. Grandma said she didn't know that she wanted it tagged with the Cales name, but she was looking it over like she was proud.

We begged and carried on until Grandma let Uncle Vertis take us for a ride, us sitting in the rumble seat and her craning her neck from the front to make sure we weren't flung to our deaths on the sharp red dog covering the road. When Grandma wasn't hollering at us to hold on, she was hollering at him to slow down before he got the whole bunch of us killed.

Uncle Vertis looked at her and grinned.

Then he speeded up.

Although it wasn't much to look at, the two-room house Uncle Vertis and Aunt Nalda lived in was built solid enough. The living-room-bedroom didn't have room for a couch, but there were a couple of rump-sprung chairs if you had a mind to sit down in there. Most people didn't. The biggest part of visiting went on around the kitchen table where folks sat on mismatched chairs, each one painted a different color with dregs of paint Uncle Vertis brought home from the dump.

The house didn't have running water, but there was a well in the yard, one that looked like the wishing wells in story books, with a bucket tied on a rope to lower into the water. A pail of that water sat on the sink, a long-handled dipper hooked over the side. Everybody drank from the same dipper and I never heard of anybody dying from it, but they might not have told me if somebody did.

Butter and milk and eggs were kept cold in a springhouse that straddled the icy creek burbling along at the foot of the mountain.

If you'd had good hunting, the meat, kept chilled in the spring-house, was breaded in crumbs or dipped in egg and milk and flour and fried up in a greased iron skillet for supper, and what wasn't eaten was stored by salting or smoking or canning it.

The outhouse, situated downstream, was wallpapered with pictures of flowers Aunt Nalda cut from seed catalogs. Teasel and jewelweed and lobelia and phlox faded and withered on winter walls, only to be replaced by a new crop of fuchsia, dahlias, forsythia, and begonias from next spring's catalogs. A bucket of lime with a tin cup sat in the corner, and a cup or two sprinkled into the hole kept the stench down and the flies away. If money and toilet paper ran out at the same time, a page or two of the Sears, Roebuck came in handy.

When Vonnie and I got to stay with Uncle Vertis and Aunt Nalda for a week or so in the summer, we slept on a featherbed pallet on the kitchen floor and took our baths outdoors in a galvanized tub with water heated lukewarm by the sun. Aunt Nalda made picnics for us, serving our breakfast of oatmeal and brown sugar on the bridge that spanned the creek, and our midday dinner of tomato sandwiches and hardboiled eggs in the back of Uncle Vertis's truck or on the flat rock near the garden—first making us find the eggs she'd hidden in unlikely places in the yard.

And it wasn't even Easter.

Aunt Nalda helped us make paper dolls that looked like Grandma and Grandpa and Mother and everybody else in our family, with a whole wardrobe for each one. Sometimes she'd do silly things like put Grandpa's paper pants on the grandma and Grandma's bonnet on the grandpa.

She cut lengths of an old clothesline to use as jumping ropes and held one end while we learned to jump with first one, then two ropes at a time. She knew where to find teaberries and the first johnnie-jump-ups. She melted slivers of soap and water into a slimy mixture and showed us how to blow giant bubbles through a coat hanger twisted into a circle.

She pinched off pieces of the slippery yellow clay that streaked along the creek bank to make heads for dolls, poking the top of a cross made of sticks up the neck of each grinning skull before lining them up to bake their brainless heads in the sun. We fashioned crepe-paper clothes for the one-legged dolls—shawls and sashes and turbans to wear with gypsy skirts of many layers and colors, stretched to flounce at the hem to hide their infirmities.

Sissy and I sat on the logs that bridged the creek behind Uncle Vertis's house, dangling our feet above the icy water, fishing with strings and safety pins baited with scraps of fatback rind. There were minnows, of course, and trout if we were lucky, and there were other silvery little fish we called ghosts because we never caught any. We didn't this time either, nothing but a crawdad or two.

We weren't catching anything and were bored, so we asked Mother if we could walk up the road to the backside of the mountain, which at least had a chance of leading to something interesting. Mother said we could, but not before she gave us a list of don't do thisses and don't do thats.

Uncle Vertis caught up with us, well out of sight of the women back at the house. They would have had a conniption if they had known what he was up to, ever last one of them. He handed me the bag Boo had brought the moonshine in. A ragged shoelace was tied around the top with a double knot so I couldn't open it, although I did try.

"Now there's no need to get your grandma all worked up, so keep this little bit of business between you and me and Missy," Uncle Vertis said, after asking me to drop the bag off at Boo's place.

"It's Sissy," I told him. "Her name's Sissy."

"Just as well not mention it to any of the womenfolk back at the house," he said again, like he didn't think I understood him the first time. "If they get their dander up, feathers are likely to fly," he said, tucking his hands under his armpits and flapping his elbows like wings. He folded my hand around a quarter he'd dug out of his pocket.

I knew it was a bribe.

I took it anyway.

"You go and buy you and Missy a bottle of soda pop or one of them ice creams." Uncle Vertis turned to head back toward the house.

"Her name's Sissy," I hollered after him.

Uncle Vertis flapped his wings.

"Turn around before you get to the Galway Place," Mother had said. So we did, three times for good measure. "And don't be writing your name on anybody's car," she'd added. We didn't. Instead we wrote KILROY WAS HERE in the dust on cars parked close enough to the road that we wouldn't get caught.

Narrower and less tended the higher it went, the road dead-ended at the top of the mountain. Just stopped sudden, like there was no place past that particular point anybody would ever have the need to go. Boo Boudreaux lived at the end of that road. To get there we had to pass the old Galway place, empty for years. Although we'd never worked up the nerve to go inside, we were somehow drawn to the idea of ghosts or dead bodies. Uncle Vertis claimed he'd seen strange lights inside many a night. "Galway's ghost most likely," he'd said, making his black eyes big and scary.

Grandma told him there was no such thing as ghosts and he was to stop filling our heads with such foolishness because she was getting awful tired of having to cut the lights on before we went upstairs to bed every night and make no mistake about it he was squarely to blame for putting that fear in us and here he was a grown man and ought to be ashamed of himself scaring little children out of their wits.

Uncle Vertis listened to every word, nodding like he agreed. Then he'd made his hands into monster claws and chased us halfway to Sunday.

Grandma just shook her head.

The Galway place went out of its way to make you believe it was haunted. Weeds and brush had taken over most of the yard, and the outhouse had been tipped over, probably by kids some long-ago Halloween. The house sat at the end of a dirt lane that was barely passable. We picked our way through the bramble as far as the falling-down porch. Morning glories, their purple trumpets blaring silently into the sun, threaded around and through the broken porch rail and sagging shutters. I pulled one of the plants out by the roots to give to Aunt Nalda, wrapping it in damp leaves to keep it alive like I'd seen her do.

We stopped at the porch. Even though Sissy dared me and called me a scaredy-cat, I refused to go inside.

"You go," I said, calling her bluff.

"I will if you will," she said.

We both chickened out.

We started around the house, her in the lead. It's what we always ended up doing, hoping bigger hoodlums than us had torn the boards off a window so we could stand on our tiptoes and look inside, but nobody had, at least not yet.

Sissy stopped, turning to shush me. She pointed to a contraption of pipes and kettles almost hidden by the forest. Although busted-up stills were scattered all over these mountains, I'd never seen one that looked ready to run. We were turning to leave when we heard the sound of something clanging against metal over and over again.

Hunched over, Sissy and I backtracked out of there, sneaking looks over our shoulders to make sure nobody was after us with a double-barrel shotgun that could take both of us down with one scattered blast. When we got to the road, we took off running and didn't let up until we both got a stitch and had to catch our breath, bending over like hunchbacks to clutch at the sharp pain in our sides. As soon as we could straighten up, we ran the rest of the way to Boo's house. His wife, dark and sharp-featured like him, was sitting on the porch nursing a baby that looked to be two or three years old. She was singing a song.

Just as we got to the porch Boo pulled up in his car. I noticed the door handle was missing. I'd heard somebody say, Uncle Vertis maybe, that moonshiners took the handles off to make it hard for the law to get in. It was a dead giveaway somebody was a real moonshiner, not just running an occasional batch of shine for his family and friends.

Boo walked over, swinging a ball-peen hammer in his hand. "Where in tarnation y'all pick up all them beggar-lice?"

He seemed a little too interested to me. But then again, that could have been my nerves working on me. I looked down. The daisy-flowered pedal pushers Grandma had made from feed sacks were covered with the flat sticky seeds that grew in a pod almost like a green pea. I swiped at them a couple of times, but it did little good. Beggar-lice had to be picked off one-by-one-by-one. Sissy had them all over her pants too.

So did Boo Boudreaux.

The hair on my arms prickled up. I was scared Boo had seen us back at the Galway place, and here I was standing in front of him sweating and out of breath and covered up to my waist in beggar-lice. Oh, I had guilty written all over me. And Sissy just stood there saying nothing, like her face didn't even have a mouth on it.

"My Uncle Vertis asked me to give you this," I handed Boo the sack without answering about the beggar-lice.

Boo pulled a switchblade out of his pants and snapped it open. Around the hilt was a dark rusty color that could have been dried-up squirrel or rabbit blood or even rust for all I knew. On the other hand, it could have been from whatever fight caused that slope of scar on his face. He ran a callused finger along the edge of the knife. Judging it sharp enough, he slashed the shoestring the bag was tied with, shaking a couple bills and some change into his hand.

Picking out a quarter, he handed it to me. "You girls look like you could use a pop. It's hotter than a hound in heat today."

Of course I knew the right thing to do.

Instead, I took the money.

With his black hair, bandana, and that knife glinting in the sun, Boo looked like a pirate. His wife started singing "Power in the Blood," the baby still nursing at her breast. *"There is power, wonder working power, in the blood of the Lamb,"* her voice softly keening. *"Power, power, wonder working power, in the precious blood of the lamb,"* she sang, never once looking up or saying a word to any of us. The child unlatched from her breast and yawned, showing a full set of baby teeth. Milk dribbled down its chin.

"You tell your uncle it's a pleasure doing business with him," Boo said. "And tell him I'll be returning that hammer of his next time I come down. Everything's working slick as snot."

Sissy and I had got ourselves into a situation. Practically getting yourself shot by a moonshiner wasn't near as much fun if you couldn't tell about it, fancying it up with each telling.

But we couldn't tell a solitary soul.

Not about going on the Galway property. Or seeing the moonshine still. Or taking the quarter from Uncle Vertis or Boo either. We couldn't even say we'd talked to Boo. Since either bragging or confessing was likely to get us in trouble with one or the other of them, I thought the best way to deal with our sins was to keep our mouths shut and put the money in the offering at church on Sunday. Before I could fully plead my case, Sissy took the quarters and threw them as far as she could into the weeds.

"What the heck did you do that for?" I asked.

"St. Mary's doesn't want moonshine money," Sissy said, just like she had asked the Methodists about it the last time she was there.

I hoped she wouldn't blab to anybody at church about us taking moonshine money from Boo. We'd disgraced ourselves enough that folks were likely still talking about it. A few weeks back the two of us had sung "Fairest Lord Jesus" for morning service, but the music was so loud I couldn't hear Sissy and I doubted she could hear me. I know we sounded awful because Patty Greer told me so. She was one of my best friends, and that is something she would not lie about.

I was still fuming about Sissy throwing the money away. If she didn't want to give it to the Lord, the least she could have done was give it back to me. I didn't talk to her all the way home. She kept trying to get me to slow down, but I'd got it in my head that Boo had seen us snooping around at the Galway place. I kept looking back to make sure he wasn't chasing us, waving a ball-peen hammer in one hand and a bloody knife in the other, lunging closer with every step he took.

When we got back to the house, Aunt Nalda and Uncle Vertis had been in a fuss over him buying moonshine from Boo right there in broad daylight with Grandma not much more than spitting distance away. Besides, the egg money Aunt Nalda kept hidden in her sewing basket was short two dollars and fifty-three cents. Uncle Vertis was a little drunk, but not drunk enough to admit he'd been into Aunt Nalda's egg money and spent it on moonshine.

"Nobody but a sorry-no-good-for-nuthin' would steal a good Christian woman's egg money," he said.

"That same no-good-for-nuthin' better see it gets put back in there." Aunt Nalda gave him a steely look. "Just to make sure, I'm keeping that saw you borrowed from Boo until it does."

I'd heard Grandma tell Mother if Aunt Nalda wanted Uncle Vertis to quit drinking, she needed to stop nagging about it. "Nagging would drive anybody to drink," she said. "And a man with a weakness for alcohol didn't stand a chance." Grandma took the boy's side in most everything. "You get yourself right with the Lord and He'll convict you of drinking that poison," Grandma told Uncle Vertis. He hated to be preached at, so she snuck it in a little at a time like doses of medicine.

Uncle Vertis said maybe one day he'd up and quit cold turkey, but he didn't feel the need just yet. Sprawled on a salvaged car seat that was part of a matched set being used for porch furniture, he put his head back, pulled his hat down, and closed his eyes against the sun.

We finished up the molasses making, the last a boiling of black-strap, before we drove the few miles home, our plans for going to the pines abandoned because of the moonshine and the commotion about it. Aunt Nalda invited us back the next day to make up for it.

"I figure we might as well eat up that watermelon we got chilling in the springhouse," she said. "Only the women going this time. Your uncle is likely to be a tad under the weather."

I was real mad about that. If Uncle Vertis wasn't there, who would kill a snake if I happened across one? Or carry me down the mountain if I broke my leg? The next day Aunt Lila and Vonnie decided to go with us, but Grandma stayed home. She said the strawberries needed tending, but I knew it was because of Uncle Vertis buying that moonshine. It wasn't fair. Grandma was needed to keep me out of the poison ivy and to rub the fur off my peach. It was Uncle Vertis's fault, every bit of it, and I wasn't about to forgive him.

The next day Grandma made flapjacks for breakfast so we could try out the newly jarred blackstrap we'd brought home. Grandpa, who hadn't had much of an appetite lately, managed to eat part of one. It was, he declared, the absolute best blackstrap he'd ever put in his mouth.

"Oh Clev, you always say that," Grandma said.

Grandpa was having a bad day, he'd had a lot of them lately, and it dawned on me that was why Grandma was staying home. Once I figured that out, I was glad she wasn't going with us, but it scared me too. It was the first time I ever thought the bellyaches could kill my grandpa. That he could actually die had never crossed my mind.

We drove back to Daniels and climbed up the mountain to the pines, all of us acting extra jokey. We ate our picnic of meatloaf sandwiches and watermelon, the women sitting on the ground and talking while me and Vonnie slid halfway down the mountain on cardboard we'd brought home from Calloway's grocery store.

"Your uncle fixed up a surprise I'm supposed to show you girls."
Aunt Nalda walked us to a clearing where a swing hung from high
in a lone pine tree.

Higher and higher I pumped. I could see the house and truck
and make out the line the creek drew around the foot of the mountain. Flapjack, grazing in high pasture halfway up the mountain,
swatted at flies with his hairless tail. But here, upwind of him, the
air tasted of pine and of the cloyed sweet of decaying trees.

Higher and higher.

The mountain fell away beneath my feet.

All the Bells
Were Ringing

There was a pall came over 211 Bibb Avenue the day my grandpa died. I don't know how I knew, but I did, that life as I'd known it since I had memory was to change on that day. I was twelve years old.

The bellyaches that doubled him over had worsened. Finally, because the doctors didn't know what else to try, they split him open gullet to guts. "Full of cancer," they told Grandma. Nothing to do but sew the strangely crooked gash back together with a coarse dark thread. We brought him, weak and wounded, home to die.

Grandma put him in the guest bedroom downstairs, the one where his mother died years earlier, the one usually reserved for visiting preachers and missionaries. He lay in the big poster bed enduring pain that was unendurable.

I sang his favorite hymns. I talked to him about the almanac and the new kittens and Queenie and Bossy and the extra warm weather. I refreshed his pitcher of water and refilled his coffee cup. I read Scripture to him every morning and the *Raleigh Register* every afternoon, skipping the obituaries, of course. I sat in the dark of night and held his hand.

The truth is, I did none of those things.

I couldn't bear to go into that room, not unless I had to. When I heard him moaning, I'd holler for Grandma. I'm not proud of that, but I just couldn't.

Grandpa reached for the brown bottle of Hadacol on the bedside table. He unscrewed the cap and took a deep pull, shuddering as he swallowed it down. Hadacol was advertised everywhere—on the radio and in the newspaper and on signs along the road—and claimed to cure a whole bunch of ailments. Grandma said that Sister Wood said it helped her neighbor who was afflicted with crippling arthritis, so Grandpa agreed to give it a try. Since the Hadacol eased his misery better than anything so far, Grandma kept a bottle on hand, although the $3.50 price was sometimes hard to come by.

One afternoon Grandma was reading the newspaper to Grandpa when an article caught her eye. The makers of Hadacol were being forced to stop claiming it could cure everything from asthma to sinking spells because they couldn't prove a bit of it. They'd got away with it by saying it was a tonic, not a medicine, and it did contain vitamin B and some other things that were supposed to be good for you.

But it was the next line that got them both stirred up.

Hadacol, she read, was twelve percent alcohol. Why, it was even being served up in shot glasses in some beer joints—it said so right there in black and white.

No doubt about it, my teetotaler grandpa was a boozer, albeit unknowingly.

And Lord help her, my teetotaler grandma was supplying him with the booze.

Even though a couple swigs of Hadacol gave him a blessed few hours of relief, from then on Grandpa refused to touch a drop. I watched Grandma turn the bottle upside down over the sink until it was empty, her mouth set.

During the warm spring evenings, we played croquet on the strip of lawn beside the house—me and Vonnie, Sissy, and the young couple from across the street. Sissy's red-striped mallet hit the matching wooden ball and skittered my green one across the clipped lawn, ricocheting off the side of the house.

Thwack.

Mother came out on the porch and stood watching for a minute, her head stiff like it might fall right off her neck. Her green eyes were dark with suffering. I could tell she had The Headache. I capitalized it in my mind because it wasn't just any old run-of-the-mill headache. It was the one that sent her to bed for three or four days, hunkered under the covers to escape the light.

"Y'all can't be making all that noise. The racket's bothering your grandpa," she said, never mentioning that it wasn't doing her headache any good either, but then she'd never been one to complain.

Although we were careful to steer the balls away from the house, before long another one would go astray.

Whomp.

And she'd appear again, green chenille robe clutched around her.

"Okay, that's enough for tonight. It's getting too dark out to see anyway."

We'd have a molasses cookie and a glass of milk before heading up the stairs to bed.

"You two better get your britches down here and brush your teeth before you go another step," Mother scolded, her face smeared white with cold cream.

We climbed onto the banister, saying, "Yes ma'am," as we slid past her.

"You know your grandma's gonna skin you alive if she catches you doing that," she said, wiping her face with a clean white rag.

She bent over to brush her hair a hundred strokes, so we could tell her headache was easing off. We ran to the top of the stairs to slide down again.

"Okay, but that better be the last time," she warned. "And don't anybody come running to me if they break a leg," she added without looking up.

"We can't come running if we break a leg," Vonnie said.

"Well, it wouldn't do you any good if you could."

At night, when the house was quiet except for the moans and occasional snores coming from Grandpa's room, I'd lie in bed, eyes closed, and see him, peart and wiry, going about his day, me tucking along behind.

There we are, out hoeing the garden—him at one end of a row and me at the other. He steps off a ten foot square and puts a stake at each corner.

"That's your garden," he tells me, "and you can plant anything you want long as you tend it."

I choose leaf lettuce and green onions, yellow tomatoes and little red tommy-toes. I dig and plant and weed and fertilize. When my garden comes in, Grandpa lets me pick the salad makings for dinner.

"Looky here what this little handful of girl did," he says. "Why, them boys larping around over at the drug store can't hold a candle to her."

I see us sitting in the back yard, swigging lemonade from jelly jars.

When I say we're larping around, Grandpa says oh no, what we are doing is way different from those boys. "Larping," he says, "is aimless lazy, while ours is rest we earned by hoeing rows of beans." And if anybody doubted us, we'd just show them our hands. "See there," he'd say, opening my hand up in his, "me and you have the calluses to prove it."

Next I'm plaiting a little braid in his hair, right on top, and tying it with a red ribbon. It's soon time to leave for Wednesday prayer meeting, so he puts on his hat and we head out.

When he takes his hat off at the church door, Grandma's face blanches. "For land's sake," she says, "what on earth will that child think of next?"

"I wouldn't venture to guess," Grandpa replies, shaking his head.

Grandma hurries to undo my handiwork before the red ribbon calls attention and she's forever disgraced by my foolishness.

As the scenes slow to match my breathing, Grandpa is passing his hat for a visiting preacher. Sister Wood, Grandma's best friend and the church treasurer, asks him why he takes collections for every preacher and missionary coming through when he won't take a penny for himself, not even for gas money.

"We've got enough for all of our needs and some of our wants and plenty to share with those who don't. Seems to me we're making it just fine without it," Grandpa tells her.

When I wake up, there is a change to the order of things. Grandma isn't up to her elbows in flour. There's no smell of ham frying and coffee perking on the stove. Mother and Grandma hover over Grandpa all morning, watching the quilt covering him quiver with each raggedy exhale. Time ticks by, unmarked except for listening for his next breath. There is a pause in the breathing, then another breath, a gasp really.

Then the breath I keep waiting for doesn't come.

Doc Cunningham comes and goes, his worn stethoscope hanging limp from his neck, the black electrical tape Mother used to repair it for him months ago starting to come undone. Grandma and Mother come out of the bedroom crying.

"He's dead," Grandma says. The words strangle in her throat.

She wipes her worn face with a wadded-up handkerchief, then closes her eyes and takes a deep breath, straightens her back and walks to the kitchen and puts the coffee on the stove to perk. She pulls her mixing bowl and breadboard from the cupboard and begins the task that has started her days for the past fifty years. And while the biscuits bake, she waits for the funeral home to come for Grandpa.

The air is thin and sticky as spider webs. I can't suck enough of it in to keep me breathing.

I reach for Vonnie's hand and pull her outside.

We sit in the back yard, the place we call the park, bare toes pushing into the patch of earth beneath the swing to keep it going a little. I close my eyes and I'm sitting there with Grandpa, my feet scuffing the ground. "You'll never get anywhere in life if you drag your feet," he says.

Two of the neighbor ladies, ones I don't know too well, come to the back door and start to knock. They notice us in the swing and one calls out. "We's just wantin' to know how the mister is doing." Her voice jars into the utter despair I have no words for.

"He's dead," I manage to answer, repeating Grandma's words.

I remember feeling sorry for those women, dressed in their visiting clothes, ones that were not quite church-worthy, but still too good for every day. They probably said things meant to make us feel better, about how he's in a better place now, or at least he won't have to suffer anymore, but I don't remember any of it. What I remember is how fast they managed to get away from our house, away from the scene they'd blundered into, away from death. I couldn't blame them. I didn't want to be there either.

When I close my eyes that night, there's my grandpa again, squirting milk from Bossy, our Jersey cow, straight into my mouth, me squealing for him to stop—no, do it again!

We're in the woods together. Grandpa's chopping down a Christmas tree and dragging it to the car.

Next, he's saying grace at the kitchen table.

"Lord, we just thank you for this food that we are about to receive and ask that you use it to the nourishment of our bodies. We pray in the blessed name of Jesus. Amen."

It could have been dinner or supper, maybe breakfast, I forgot to notice what was heaped on the platters, but it doesn't matter, because he said grace every meal.

Grandpa, smelling of Bossy and Old Spice, is walking me to school in a snowstorm, and without him saying so, I know he'll be waiting there to walk me home.

There he is preaching at a revival, his Bible held up to the heavens, his voice reaching to the far corners of the tent. "Amen!" he shouts, his voice soaring over the congregation. "The Lord is raining down His glory as we're gathered here to worship Him tonight! Yes sir! He's raining down His glory! Let's praise Him as we turn to page 384 in our hymnal and sing 'There Will Be Showers of Blessing.'"

I see him with hobos or gypsy boys or with a bag of squirrels he's brought home from a hunting trip, dumping them on the ground for me and Vonnie to pick the best tails to hang from our bike handles. "They's a pair of red ones in there oughta match up real nice," he tells us.

The sitting room off the bedroom Grandpa died in served to hold the casket for the viewing. People brought food to the house to last for days, and still Grandma cooked more. A ham with rings of cinnamon apples tacked on with cloves. A pot of green beans and new potatoes seasoned with fatback. A platter of fried chicken. Mother made tomato dumplings and deviled eggs and a blackberry cake to serve with fresh whipped cream. A pan of her yeast rolls went into the oven.

Vonnie and I took our plates out to the swing to eat. Away from all those people who were either talking too much or not at all. Away from the bedroom where Grandpa died. Away from the casket where my Grandpa was laid out in a dark gray suit, his stilled hands folded on the satin coverlet.

The bells of St. Mary's Methodist joined those of Wildwood Community Church and the Pentecostal Holiness Church my grandpa preached at in East Beckley. Pastor Parker from Wildwood Community preached the funeral. He and Grandpa were, according to his words on that day, "brothers in Christ."

Grandpa had opened our door to him just after dark one night. The big man stood there, shrunken and trembling, sorrow ravaging his face. "She was so little," Pastor Parker said, "so very little. Like a baby bird." He wasn't driving fast or anything. She ran right out from between two cars. It happened so fast, he remembered only a blur of yellow. Her corn-tassel hair, maybe, or her sundress. He couldn't be sure. But as God was his witness, there was nothing he could do—he'd give his life if there was.

Of course he would, and no, there was not a thing he could do. "She's an angel in Heaven now," Grandpa told him, "safe in the arms of Jesus."

They talked often after that, and they prayed, and finally they laughed.

Grandpa told Pastor Parker he believed he could make a fair-to-middlin' Pentecostal out of him if he had enough time.

"I wouldn't be holding my breath if I was you," Pastor Parker replied. "You're invited, though, to warm a pew at Wildwood Community anytime you've a notion to."

"Well, don't put my name on one just yet," Grandpa said.

The little church filled up, then people crowded the steps and the grounds. People came from all around. W. W. Carter, Superintendent of the Pentecostal Holiness Church, came. He had stayed at our house many times, was almost like family. He taught me how to read before I started school.

The whole congregation, or so it seemed, came from Cales Chapel, the church Grandpa and Grandma founded in Coal City.

Cecil Miller came. He was the principal of Sylvia Elementary School, where Sissy Moles and Peggy Blevins and Patty Greer and I would be eighth-grade cheerleaders in the fall, and I would be co-valedictorian with Bill Grose in the spring. They all came. And so did David Stanley and Tony Cox, a couple of neighborhood boys I'd known since first grade. On rainy days they chased us home from school with the slimy fat earthworms that oozed up from the mud and stretched a foot long from their grimy fists, sometimes squeezing the insides out like pink toothpaste. Both sides went slower or faster to keep what we judged a safe distance between us. The rules were unspoken and unwritten. Yet somehow we all knew how to play the game.

I don't remember much about the service, but at the end the choir sang a doleful rendition of one of Grandpa's favorite hymns, "Will the Circle Be Unbroken." There was an invitation for folks to come forward to confess their sins and receive eternal salvation, and I like to think a sinner or two answered the call. The funeral director closed the casket, lined with pearl-gray satin, over my grandpa's face, and the pallbearers, Uncle Ed and Uncle Cliff and others from the church, came forward to carry him away.

Cars on both sides of the highway pulled over and turned on their lights as mourners in Chevrolets and Plymouths and Fords followed a black hearse and cars filled with flowers to the cemetery.

So many flowers.

"Flowers are for the living," Grandma says, so she has most of them delivered to Pinecrest Sanitarium, a huge brick building where people with tuberculosis were quarantined and treated, sometimes for years. "Besides, that's what your grandpa would want me to do."

As the hearse carrying my grandpa arrived at an open grave on a gentle rise, the last car pulled onto the funeral grounds. I watched the black iron gates of Sunset Memorial Cemetery swing shut behind us.

Epilogue: we are going home . . .

And the end of all our exploring
Will be to arrive where we started
And know the place for the first time.

T. S. Eliot

Fifty-five years after Grandpa's death Sissy and I drive through the black wrought-iron gates and up the rise to the gravesite. We stand at the foot of my grandpa's grave. Humbled and small, I am in the presence of greatness.

"I will lift up mine eyes unto the hills, from whence cometh my strength."

The mountains fold around me.

The marble tombstone is elegant. That's Grandma's doing.

Luther Clevland Cales 7.7.1877—7.30.1952

Grandma's name and date of birth are also cut into the stone:

Clerrinda Adkins Cales 9.12.1887

But Grandma isn't buried next to Grandpa. She's lived in Florida for more than four decades and decides that's where she will stay. "Be easier on the family," she tells me. Since most of us have migrated to Florida, I nod like I agree.

I am holding her hand when Grandma dies on December 14, 1990, at age one hundred three and a half. We bury her next to Vertis, the second of her sons to be buried before her—the first an infant boy—where her two daughters, my mother, Iva Kathleen, and aunt, Lila Lora, will be buried in time. Years later, I consider moving her to the gravesite next to Grandpa, having the date she died carved into the stone. I decide against it. She made her decision, and I will continue to honor it.

But as the heir next in line, I can be buried there. Two people can if they are cremated, which is what my husband and I have planned. An old rhyme comes to mind,

> I'm a West Virginian born and bred,
> and I'll be a West Virginian when I'm dead.

Terry is a native Pennsylvanian. I ask how he feels about being buried in West Virginia. "That'd make you a bona fide, dirt-dyed hillbilly," I tell him.

"I'm going wherever you go," he says.

"All right then. We're going home."

The last four generations of the unbroken chain of women in my family—my mother, me, my daughter, my granddaughter—are together at my mother's home in Florida for what will be the last time. Mother, who never smoked, is dying of lung cancer. She is cold, so I go to a closet and pull down a quilt. Behind it is a small brass-trimmed cedar box, meant for storing trinkets or jewelry or memories. I use an old wire coat hanger to retrieve it from the back of the shelf. Mother says it was Grandma's, so Rindy immediately claims it for herself. She asserts ownership of anything once owned by this great-great-grandma whose name she carries. She shakes the box, then opens it. It is empty. She turns it over. There is an inscription, printed in Grandma's uneven scrawl:

TO RINDY FROM HER GRANDMA IN HEAVEN

We all laugh and cry at the same time, reminding me once again of the joyful sound of Pentecostals praying. Grandma's presence is with us in the room.

She visits me sometimes, turning lights on and off to get my attention. Signs from her appear everywhere I go, and I follow her footprints to unexpected places.

I see her looking down on us, and she is laughing.

She turns to Grandpa, "Looks like they found the memory box."
He smiles and shakes his head. "Sure took them long enough."

Now and again, when autumn days crisp like a Winesap and the stars line up just so, the trees fluoresce into brilliance. And when they do, I am grateful to bear witness. As the last faded leaf falls from the cherry tree, scabby limbs are bared to the cold. Night skies come earlier and blacker, lit by stars that glitter like diamonds.

We are in the waning days of such a season.

I think back to tent meetings and dinners on the ground, to sugar water on my pigtails, and old hymns floating on soft mountain air.

Faces and voices and sweet sacred places turn in my head.

My eyes click open.

Grandma says, "Don't you be running on that red dog road."

But I do.

I run wild, whooping and yowling against the pale November sky.

Amen.

Acknowledgments

My heartfelt thanks to . . . Grandpa and Grandma Cales for being the best teachers I ever had. They taught me that the gift is in the giving. That I should put myself neither above nor beneath anyone. That the world is a good place already and I should try to make it better. I give them credit for most of the good in me.

My mother Kathleen for buying us a home and fixing the roof and the washing machine herself. For taking me to open my own savings account when I started school. Brainy, responsible—a remarkable role model. She was skilled and talented and an artist in everything she did.

Aunt Lila for her unfailing good humor. For giving me stories like *Lonely Hearts Club Man* and *Birds of a Feather*. Entreprenurial, artistic—a lover of flowers and books and art.

My brother Hursey Clev, *Brooksville Star* newspaper, and sister, Yvonne Elaine, Ohio high school teacher—may you both rest in peace. My only surviving sibling, my brother Steve, still in West Virginia—I wish you joy and love and peace.

My husband, Terry, for listening as I struggled to give voice to the flesh and bones of kin rattling through my Appalachian blood. For unfailing patience and support. For eating cereal for dinner more often than I will admit to in writing.

My son, Carey, and grandsons C.J. and Andrew. My daughter, Andrea, and granddaughters Rindy and Camy. My great-grandchildren— Drema, Hunter and Lila, Daisy and Cindy, and all who come after. I wrote this book for you. Hold each other close. When times are tough, it's nice to know someone has your back. Live your best life. One day your grandchild might write a book about you.

Myrna Moles is the Sissy in my stories. Best friends from age three, she encouraged me to write this book and stayed with me to the bittersweet end. We talked for countless hours, unearthing her memories and mine, agreeing on this, disagreeing on that—sometimes I let her win, sometimes she let me. Over the mountains and through the valleys, she was always there.

Peggy Blevins, Patty Greer, Myrna Moles, (and me), the fearless foursome who shared Girl Scouts, cheerleading, and secrets—and countless hours talking about all those cute East Beckley boys—Steve Bibb, Bill Grose, Grant Slack, David Stanley, and all the rest.

Ruth Hoffman (deceased), revered English teacher, Hernando High School, Brooksville, Florida, 1953–54, was the first to tell me I had the makings of a writer.

Herbert Kiser, honored journalism teacher, Woodrow Wilson High School, Beckley, West Virginia, 1956–57. He believed in me back then and still does. A role model, a mentor, a shining example.

The Writers Garret, home of our renowned Dallas writing community, allowed me to grow in the heady company of other writers. Saturday mornings in the upper room with Mark Noble's Stone Soup group was an almost spiritual experience.

Kathleen Rodgers, great friend and author of two award-winning novels, rescued me from the Harpies when they took over, and applauded loudly when I put a couple good sentences together. Tom clapped too.

Marcia Cooper, friend, performer, and writer, arranged many of my speaking events. She carried copies of my stories everywhere she went, sharing them with too many captive audiences to count.

Nancy Stewart, then editor of the *Register Herald's Divine* magazine, published several of my stories. Lisa Shrewsberry, former *WV South* editor, published many others, and Brenda Pinnell, former *WV South* art director, brought them to life with her whimsical illustrations.

ACKNOWLEDGMENTS

Bill Marvel, Juli McCullagh, Robin Underdahl (and Judith Greene Emeritus), all published award-winning authors and members of Salon Quatre, our fierce Dallas writing group. After spending a day in their company, I am encouraged, inspired, humbled.

A special thank you to my agent, Jeanie Loiacono, Loiacono Literary Agency, for connecting me with Zondervan. Thank you to David Morris, Zondervan Trade Publisher, for your interest in my book. And thank you to the amazing team at Zondervan—Stephanie Smith, Bob Hudson, Alicia Kasen, Bridgette Brooks, Jennifer Ver Hage, Bridget Harmon, and all the others—for believing in *Running on Red Dog Road* and helping me make it better every step of the way.

Many others helped me hold my dream in my hand. Named or unnamed, I love you all.